Supertramp
Crime of the Century

Steve Pilkington

sonicbondpublishing.com

Sonicbond Publishing Limited
www.sonicbondpublishing.co.uk
Email: info@sonicbondpublishing.co.uk

First Published in the United Kingdom 2024
First Published in the United States 2024

British Library Cataloguing in Publication Data:
A Catalogue record for this book is available from the British Library

ISBN 978-1-78952-327-0

Typeset in ITC Garamond Std & ITC Avant Garde Gothic
Printed and bound in England

Graphic design and typesetting: Full Moon Media

Follow us on social media:
Twitter: https://twitter.com/SonicbondP
Instagram: www.instagram.com/sonicbondpublishing_/
Facebook: www.facebook.com/SonicbondPublishing/

Linktree QR code:

Acknowledgements

Thanks as always to Stephen Lambe and the whole of the Sonicbond organisation for continuing to have faith in my work – the cheque is, metaphorically, in the post!

Thanks to Janet for being a hugely supportive help and sounding board as always, acting in a 'quality control' capacity and pointing out the gremlin-introduced typos which always appear...

Thanks to the person at school in 1974 who first lent me a copy of *Crime Of The Century*. His identity has escaped my memory, but the initial reaction I had to hearing the album has never left me.

Huge thanks, in particular, to Roger Hodgson, who was generous enough to give me a substantial amount of his time when speaking with me in 2012 and 2014 for features which appeared in the magazine *Rock Society*, published at the time by the Classic Rock Society. He was patient, good-humoured and enormously easy to get along with.

Naturally, thanks also must go to the other members of the band down the years, but particularly, the 'classic five', who recorded the albums from *Crime Of The Century* through to ... *Famous Last Words...*.

Finally, thanks to you, whoever you may be, for reading this book. I hope it brings you enjoyment and interest!

Would you like to write for Sonicbond Publishing?

We are mainly a music publisher, but we also occasionally publish in other genres including film and television. At Sonicbond Publishing we are always on the look-out for authors, particularly for our two main series, On Track and Decades.

Mixing fact with in depth analysis, the On Track series examines the entire recorded work of a particular musical artist or group. All genres are considered from easy listening and jazz to 60s soul to 90s pop, via rock and metal.

The Decades series singles out a particular decade in an artist or group's history and focuses on that decade in more detail than may be allowed in the On Track series.

While professional writing experience would, of course, be an advantage, the most important qualification is to have real enthusiasm and knowledge of your subject. First-time authors are welcomed, but the ability to write well in English is essential.

Sonicbond Publishing has distribution throughout Europe and North America, and all our books are also published in E-book form. Authors will be paid a royalty based on sales of their book.

Further details about our books are available from www.sonicbondpublishing.com. To contact us, complete the contact form there or email info@sonicbondpublishing.co.uk

Supertramp
Crime of the Century

Contents

Introduction

Crime Of The Century. Is it Supertramp's finest album? Ask a hundred Supertramp fans that question, and while you will get plenty of votes for, say, *Even In The Quietest Moments* or the commercial landmark *Breakfast In America*, it's probably safe to put your mortgage on there being a large swathe of that hundred who would certainly reply in the affirmative. No album, no matter how revered, will ever move the whole of a fanbase in the same way. *Who's Next?* Well, what about *Quadrophenia? Abbey Road?* Come on now, there's *Revolver* or *Sgt Pepper. Exile On Main Street?* Well, it's no *Sticky Fingers. Led Zeppelin 4?* Let me counter that with *Physical Graffiti* ... and the discussions will go on ad infinitum. And so they should because music, even great music, is always a subjective matter.

What cannot be refuted, however, is the sheer historical or career significance of certain albums. *Dark Side Of The Moon* put Pink Floyd forever into a new, rarefied level of success. *Deep Purple In Rock* took a middlingly successful band via a lineup tweak to a whole new stylistic focus, from which they never looked back. *Led Zep 4* gave the world 'Stairway To Heaven' and launched a million radio plays. All of those albums, and many more which are probably jumping to your mind at this moment, impacted the career trajectories of the bands involved in such a way that they would never be the same again. So it was with *Crime Of The Century.*

In an even more dramatic way than some of those above examples, the *Crime* album redefined Supertramp completely in the consciousness of a public who were either unaware or largely apathetic to their previous releases. Having put out two albums searching for not only a direction but also a stable lineup, the stars aligned and the universally known 'classic' Supertramp lineup came together to record this 1974 milestone release and would remain together for almost a decade. The album saw them move instantly up several rungs on the ladder, and while they may have inched up commercially on subsequent releases, culminating with *Breakfast In America*, there was never again an ascent so rapid or so marked.

Put simply, *Crime Of The Century* 'made' Supertramp. It put them on the musical map and wrote the name in permanent marker. It opened up new global audiences for them and gave them mainstream media exposure, ranging from appearing on *The Old Grey Whistle Test* to getting a mention on the ubiquitous UK soap opera *Coronation Street!* Several tracks from the album have gone on to become genuine rock classics, while the cover itself remains utterly iconic. This book will explore what led up to the album's creation, how it was put together, the legacy it left behind and the shadow it has cast over the years. Rip off the mask, and let's see …

The Road To 'Crime'

A look at the back cover of *Crime Of The Century* reveals the expected credits and informative text, but also two words printed unobtrusively and without further explanation in the top left: 'To Sam'. This small yet significant note is a respectful nod In the direction of Dutch millionaire and early Supertramp philanthropist of sorts Stanley August Miesegaes. Known affectionately as Sam, owing to his initials, it is no stretch that he was as instrumental and as vital a cog in the early Supertramp machine as any of the musicians involved in its coming together. From the moment he first saw Rick Davies playing with a band named The Joint, in Germany in the late 1960s, it was his belief and financial support which allowed the fledgling band to keep on the road and making music.

Rick Davies was born in 1944 in Swindon, Wiltshire, with a hairdresser mother and a father in the Merchant Navy. Oddly enough, for someone who would become synonymous with playing keyboards, the first instrument which fascinated him was the drums when he was given an old radiogram at the age of seven which included a few records. One of these was a song called 'Drummin' Man' by the remarkable Gene Krupa and his orchestra, and it fired the young Davies' imagination like nothing else he had ever heard. 'It hit me like a thunderbolt', he said later. 'I must have played it 2,000 times'. Galvanised by this moment, he set out to learn to play the drums, which was his first instrument.

By 1959, he had become entranced by rock 'n' roll and, by now, was also playing the keyboards, though surprisingly, he was self-taught on that instrument as opposed to the lessons he had taken to learn the drums. The first band he joined went by the typically unimaginative name (of the time) Vince and the Vigilantes. By 1962, he was emboldened enough to start his own band for the first time, and although 'Rick's Blues' wasn't much of an improvement in terms of a band name, it was a significant landmark in his early career. Having, by now, switched to the electric piano himself, the drum stool in Rick's Blues was occupied by a young man named Ray O'Sullivan, who would go on to his own success a decade later following his own switch to piano and a change of name to Gilbert O'Sullivan. Rick had, in fact, taught Ray the drums and also the piano, and they remained friends. O'Sullivan later became the best man at Rick's wedding. Rick's Blues disbanded when Rick's father became ill, and he took a job as a welder, which he later confessed to absolutely loathing.

His musical ambitions would not be stifled, however, and in 1966, he managed to secure a place as organist in a band called The Lonely Ones. This was quite notable as he had, in fact, never played the organ in his life but assumed it would be much the same as any other keyboard and simply lied about it when applying. The Lonely Ones, at one point, included the later Jimi Hendrix Experience bassist Noel Redding, though he had already left the band by the time Rick came on board. In 1967, The Lonely Ones changed their name to the scarcely better 'The Joint' and began playing on the continent, where they would go on to provide music for several German films, which have been lost to the mists of time long ago. It was soon after this that he first encountered Sam, and his destiny was to be forever changed.

The Joint were working in Germany at the time, desperately pumping out production-line music for production-line films. This dispiriting compositional work would occupy them during the day, while scarcely more rewarding gigs took up their nocturnal hours. They were working – via the films – for a man named David Lluellyn, who Rick remembers getting them all of the movie contacts. One day, Lluellyn mentioned to the band that he knew a millionaire in Switzerland who was interested in potentially getting involved with them – an announcement which naturally sounded about as pie-in-the-sky as you could get – but since, as Rick said later, they were 'living on soup' at the time, any potential pie was worth following up on. Therefore, they gave him the go-ahead to approach this shadowy millionaire benefactor on their behalf, just on the off-chance that something would come of it, and one Saturday, Lluellyn went off to meet his Swiss Connection. Unfortunately for the band, he did not return for what Rick described as 'about three months', but when he did eventually resurface, it was with positive news. His wealthy friend was keen to meet up with them to see whether they could work together. They did, and 'Sam' Miesegaes had entered the picture.

The band enthusiastically went over to Sam's house, where they stayed for a while, discussing his ideas for them, which involved ambitious plans regarding the fusing of classical and contemporary pop music, for example. Much of this came to nothing, as by Rick's own admission, the band simply weren't really good enough to justify the faith placed in them. What he did do on a practical level, however, was to provide them with a coach to ease their transport issues. Looking back in a *Sounds* feature in 1975, Rick was to comment:

One morning, Sam phoned me up at nine o'clock in the morning and told me to have a look out of the window, and I said, 'There's nothing out there except an old coach'. He said, 'It's yours, boys', so we got in, and Andy (our singer) drove it around Finchley while we played football in the back. It's only when we started playing the Marquee that it got to be a problem. We had to park in Oxford Street, and you'd see a huge chain of people on Wardour Street carrying equipment...

This happy spell under the patronage of Sam was to be relatively short-lived for The Joint, sadly, as he elected to withdraw his support not too long after the gift of the coach. Rick Davies went to talk to him and was told that he simply didn't feel the band had the potential to fulfil his ambitions for them (something which Rick agreed with, as it happens). Davies, however, was a different matter, as Sam saw something in him that he perceived as lacking in the band as a whole. Again, in that *Sounds* piece, Rick noted that:

I went over to Sam's to try and write my own music so I could get enough confidence to start something off my own back, and I stayed there just writing. Of course, all sorts of crazy ideas popped up from Sam, like 'Rick Around The World In Eighty Tunes', whereby we'd hire a few Land Rovers and go around the world! We'd sit in an Afghanistan village and be influenced by the music and then go somewhere else. It sounded fantastic, but it wasn't real at all. So, I went back to London and I began auditioning for what was to become the first Supertramp.

The first person recruited for what would become the fledgling Supertramp – still with the financial backing of Sam, who wholeheartedly supported the project – was the man who would go on to be the other half of the band's own 'Lennon And McCartney' – Roger Hodgson. Born in Portsmouth in 1950, Roger began to forge a close relationship with his guitar as a way of whiling away the time that he spent in boarding school, and as he reached his teenage years, he added keyboards, bass and even drums to his instrumental portfolio. Interestingly, at the time that he met Rick and was enticed into the formative Supertramp stable, he had also been contracted to release a single for DJM Records, recording it under the name of Argosy for some obscure reason. DJM (Dick James Music) was to become Elton John's record label, and at the time, the still-named

Reg Dwight was doing session work and writing songs for DJM. It was, therefore, unsurprising – yet no less impressive – that the Argosy single (entitled 'Mr Boyd') featured Elton on piano. The quartet was completed by drummer Nigel Olsson and guitarist Caleb Quaye, both of whom would go on to join Elton's own band. It didn't help, as the single sank like a stone – despite the fact that Roger remembers that 'Tony Blackburn liked it'. With Argosy clearly not set for world domination any time soon, his whole attention could be directed towards the new venture with Rick.

Speaking to *Velvet Goldmine* in 2007, Roger had some interesting reflections on how his songwriting partnership with Rick developed:

> It was very much that the magic or the essence of Supertramp was the kind of yin-yang polarity of Rick's songwriting and my songwriting and our two musical styles. I mean, Rick was five years older than me, so he had grown up on the music of jazz and blues. That was his background, and that's where he gravitated towards, whereas I grew up on The Beatles and pop rock. But actually, when we played together, there was an incredible empathy between the two of us, when it was just the two of us, and it was very magical, especially earlier on when there weren't too many other people around and it was, literally, just the two of us. And I think as we developed as songwriters, we started writing, obviously, totally separately, but I think just having that competition, healthy competition, we wanted to give the best of ourselves, and having another writer in the band kind of gave that sense of competition that really did bring out the best in us.

Quite surprisingly, when Roger originally got involved with the band, his instrument was the bass – he claimed that it was his favourite instrument at the time and one that he always enjoyed playing. Davies recruited Richard Palmer on guitar, with Keith Baker completing the lineup on drums. While this was effectively the first incarnation of Supertramp, technically, it was not, as the foursome initially went by the utterly hopeless name of 'Daddy'. They do say 'what's in a name', but it is, nonetheless, somewhat difficult to imagine a string of massive-selling Daddy albums throughout the decade! Thankfully, this was short-lived, as the name Supertramp was adopted in January 1970 to avoid confusion with another band who sported the only marginally better name of Daddy Longlegs. Richard Palmer actually suggested the name, based on the book *The Autobiography Of A*

Super-Tramp by Welsh poet W. H. Davies, which tells the story of his own extraordinary life. Keith Baker also departed at this time to join Uriah Heep, who were recording their own debut album at the time. In an oddly connected way, the man he replaced as Heep's drummer was none other than Hodgson's Argosy collaborator Nigel Olsson, himself on his way to join up with Elton again. A small world at that time, it would seem ...

Bob Millar came in on drums to replace Baker, and this became the lineup which signed with A&M Records and would record the band's self-titled debut in June 1970, with the release coming a month later on 14 July. Released in a striking if not particularly artistically notable sleeve depicting a man with a flower for a head, this image is certainly noteworthy for predating Peter Gabriel's rather similar (and better known) stage costume, which made its appearance a couple of years later. While the album was simply titled *Supertramp*, there were some odd exceptions to this. In Singapore, it was named 'Surely', after the split track which bookends the album, while in Spain, it bore the rather baffling title of 'Now And Then', which implied it to be some sort of compilation album one would think. In the UK, the first pressing very strangely bore the title of 'And I'm Not Like Other' – which, in itself, makes neither logical nor grammatical sense – though even more confusingly, this was printed on the record label only and nowhere on the sleeve. In fact, this phrase came from the third track, 'Aubade'/'And I Am Not Like Other Birds Of Prey' (split into two separate tracks on that original pressing), but the lifting of the partial phrase is very difficult to grasp. The first half of that title, 'Aubade', is also something worthy of clarification; coming from the old French for 'dawn serenade', it refers to a piece of poetry which specifically welcomes or celebrates the dawn.

As can be inferred from those particular song titles, and also the fact that the song 'Surely' opens the album at only 30 seconds in length – before closing it as 'Surely (Reprise)', lasting three and a half minutes – there is an air of charming pretentiousness hanging over this album. It cannot be often that a reprise of a song lasts seven times as long as the song it returns to, and this is typical of the album, which seems to manifest an air of great importance with the almost whispered mystery of Hodgson's vocals. Even Roger himself has referred to it latterly as being 'naïve' but with 'a good mood to it'. The album was recorded at Morgan Studios, with all of the sessions taking place between midnight and 6 am, owing to the band's superstitious belief that a certain magic was to be gained from recording late at night. It is not Supertramp's greatest or most focused recording, but there is a real, early 'progressive rock' feel to it, which was never really captured by the band again, and it remains a very enjoyable listen, with tracks such as 'It's A Long Road', 'Maybe I'm A Beggar' and the lengthy 'Try Again' being particularly impressive. While Roger Hodgson takes lead vocals on every track, Richard Palmer and Rick Davies contribute occasional lead vocals along with him. It is interesting to note that Davies only takes a lead vocal credit on two songs out of the ten on the album and also that, while Davies and Hodgson composed the music (still working together at that time), Palmer wrote all of the lyrics for the album. Looking at the sophistication and importance to the band of the lyrics on *Crime* and beyond, the development from the debut is quite remarkable.

The album failed to make any impression on the charts in the UK and, in fact, was not even released in America at the time (it eventually gained a belated US release in 1977, when it almost apologetically dropped into the *Billboard* chart at 158, before making its excuses and leaving). Also leaving by the end of 1970 was Bob Millar, who, via a very short-lived interim drummer named Dickie Thomas, made way for the incoming Kevin Currie. A fifth band member also entered the picture in the shape of Dave Winthrop on flute and saxophone, who actually joined in July 1970, just as the first album was being released. Perhaps most significantly, before the recording of the second album commenced in March 1971, Richard Palmer also departed, going on to contribute lyrics to three King Crimson albums. In his place initially came former Nice guitarist Davey O'List, whose less than illustrious tenure apparently lasted all of one gig before the recruitment of Frank Farrell, who was actually a bass player. Hodgson, at this point, switched – permanently, of course – to guitar.

The second album, *Indelibly Stamped*, was released in June 1971, having been recorded at Olympic Studios in April and May. The record represented something of a stylistic shift, not only in terms of the music but also the cover artwork. In place of the quirky flower-headed man of the debut release, buyers of the second got a wraparound colour gatefold featuring the naked torso of a heavily tattooed woman – hence the *Indelibly Stamped* title. It left nothing to the imagination – so much so that in the US, A&M Records elected to place gold star stickers over the two 'focal points' of the image, while in Australia, some stores refused to stock it and others sold it in in a brown paper bag. In South Africa, meanwhile, the cover featured the title written in large, unsubtle black lettering right across the offending area. The late '60s and early '70s may have been celebrated as the time of free love and permissiveness, but the general population were seemingly not considered remotely ready for the observation of nipples! The music, similarly, was more direct than the rather fey debut album, with more of a straight rock and blues influence and no meandering epics – with the exception of the closing 'Aries', which weighs in around seven and a half minutes, everything else is around or below the five-minute mark. Some maintain the album was an improvement over its predecessor, with others claiming it to be a backward step, but most agree that it did not represent any sort of high point in the band's catalogue. In recent years, Roger Hodgson has resurrected the track 'Rosie (Had Everything Planned)' in his solo shows, but back in the 1970s, the material disappeared from the set within a couple of years without any sign of a return.

Significantly, the album credits saw a shift in vocal and compositional duties. With Palmer gone, Hodgson and Davies wrote all of the lyrics as well as the music, with the aforementioned 'Rosie' being penned by Hodgson and Farrell. This song remains the only one in the whole Supertramp catalogue with Davies receiving no writing credit, as later years saw them always credited jointly, even when writing separately. In terms of the lead vocals, out of the ten tracks on the album, Davies now takes all but four after having no solo lead vocals on the debut; of the remaining tracks, Hodgson sings three and Dave Winthrop the other. Following the release of the album, the band returned to the scene of many of their formative shows, with Rick Davies quoted in *The Supertramp Book* as saying: 'We used to get people up on the bloody stage and it was just chaos, hopping away doing about three encores … No more or fewer people would come to the next gig'.

As a further point of interest regarding the album cover, there was significant speculation and misinformation about the identity of the impressively inked model at the time. The tattoos were done by an artist named Les Skuse, who had a tattoo parlour in Bristol, England. The model was mistakenly believed to be Rusty Skuse, largely because of the names 'Billy And Rusty' displayed prominently on her arm, but it was, in fact, a tattooed lady named Marion Hollier who adorns the cover. The reason for the names was eventually clarified by her niece, who stated in response to a post on an internet tattoo forum that her aunt knew Rusty and Billy Skuse, and when she visited them on one occasion, they both tattooed their names. Marion reportedly stopped being tattooed following the death of Les in 1973.

The album was far from successful and, indeed, managed to sell even fewer copies than the first record (perhaps not helped by the adornment of stars, ugly black lettering and paper bags on the cover, one might imagine). The band kept plugging away, but over the next couple of years, all members except Davies and Hodgson drifted away, and Sam finally withdrew his financial support in October 1972. Supertramp were now financially unsupported, and with two unsuccessful albums and a fragmenting lineup to their name, something had to turn up which would pull them out of the proverbial fire. Fortunately, *Crime* would be proven to pay...

Preparing The Crime

The first new member of what would be the 'classic' lineup to arrive was bassist Dougie Thomson, replacing the departing Frank Farrell, who left the band in Spring 1972. Farrell was temporarily replaced by Nick South from Alexis Korner's band, but in July, Thomson arrived and made the position his own. Even so, he was only regarded as temporary until early 1973, at which time he was confirmed as a permanent band member.

The only Scotsman in the band, Dougie Thomson was younger than Davies or Hodgson, having been born in Glasgow in March 1951. In contrast to the elder pair and their dues-paying in bands throughout the 1960s, Thomson only began playing in a serious way in 1969, doing time in a Glasgow band named, once again uninspiringly, The Beings. In September 1971, Being turned into Going, as Thomson left to join the far more successful Alan Bown, who also featured a certain John Helliwell in their ranks. A band originally known as The Alan Bown Set, they renamed themselves The Alan Bown! (complete with an unnecessary exclamation mark) before finally settling on Alan Bown, leaving it unclear as to whether that was a solo credit for bandleader Bown or the name of the band, as in 'Alice Cooper'. Whatever the truth of the matter, though, this was to be a fairly short-lived tenure, as having released their final album, *Stretching Out,* shortly before Thomson's arrival, Alan Bown promptly broke up the band in February 1972, leaving Thomson to gravitate towards his Supertramp audition a little later. In an interview with *Sounds* in 1975, he reflected on the circumstances around his joining the band:

I was just looking around for a job to get some money, and then I saw this ad for Supertramp. Sometime before, my brother, who's one of our roadies now, had been to London and brought one of their albums back. So I was aware of them. I decided to go along and see what was happening. At this point, they had been going through some incredible audition scenes. I remember going to the Pied Bull in Islington and there were some terrible scenes. Rick was there with his crash helmet and sleeping bag. Dave Winthrop had given up hope and had gone to play pinball. Roger and Kevin were there trying to get some kind of audition sorted out. So I went in, played my two minutes and left. Roger phoned me up a couple of days later, asking me to come down to his house, and it just kind of evolved from there. It really was a strange period for the band with Dave Winthrop. Sometimes, he just wouldn't come to gigs, and then he'd turn up a couple of gigs later almost as if nothing had happened … very strange.

The next position to be changed was that of the drummer after Kevin Currie began to get a little unreliable – according to Rick in that same 1975 piece: 'We did one gig in Swansea when the drummer didn't turn up. So, Rog and I split the drumming duties between us because we needed the bread; otherwise, we'd starve. It didn't go down too badly'. Whether or not it went down all right, it was clearly not a situation which could happen regularly, and a new option presented itself in the shape of American drummer Bob Siebenberg (born in 1949 in Glendale, California, and going by the stage name of Bob C. Benberg), who was playing with the otherwise very 'English' pub rock band Bees Make Honey at the time.

Bees Make Honey supported Supertramp on a few occasions, and on the first of those, Bob remembers getting there early, seeing the Supertramp drummer and being impressed with him. However, as he put it, 'then 15 minutes later, the drummer walked in'. The man he had seen behind the kit was, in fact, the still-adept Rick Davies filling in time until the arrival of Currie! Watching Supertramp at another support gig in Birmingham, Bob stayed around to watch them, and he was very impressed. As he said in 1975, 'I thought I could get on playing with them. After that, I was putting it around that they were pretty good. The way I put it was they were the closest thing to Traffic I'd seen; they were really punchy…' (By that time, the set was mostly made up of songs from *Indelibly Stamped* and quite a bit of the material which would appear on *Crime Of The Century*, albeit in very different versions.)

As it happened, that opportunity to play with the band actually arose as, a couple of days after another shared gig in Barnet, North London, Roger Hodgson phoned Benberg and told him that their drummer was leaving and they were working towards recording a new album. In *Modern Drummer*, speaking in 2014, he offered another reflection on the state of the band when he arrived:

The band was brand new. Rick Davies and Roger Hodgson had recorded two albums previously with two different lineups without much success. There was a real feeling of optimism in the new lineup, and we jelled right away. We knew we had an interesting cast of characters and totally believed in ourselves. This was the first record with the new lineup and it felt like we could do something special. The ingredients were all there. We had label support and tons of enthusiasm.

Four-fifths of the classic lineup were now in place, but more unreliability came in the form of Dave Winthrop missing shows, and it became clear that this was another situation to be addressed, ideally with a replacement sax player. Enter Dougie Thomson again, who had the perfect man in mind from his Alan Bown days. Enter the very recognisable and very outgoing figure of John Helliwell, who would go on to become a very prominent figure on stage, with his gregarious nature leading naturally to him doing the lion's share of the between-song chat to the audiences.

Born John Anthony Helliwell in Todmorden, Yorkshire, he fell in love with both jazz and wind instrumentation after hearing clarinettist Monty Sunshine playing with Chris Barber's Jazz Band, managing to secure his first clarinet at the age of 13. Getting more into modern jazz, he got a saxophone two years later and the rest, as they say, was history. After playing in various bands in the 1960s (including one called The Dicemen, about whom he stated on his website that 'we wore 'Beatle' suits with trousers so tight we had to be lifted onto the stage'), he eventually turned professional in 1965 with the bizarrely named Jugs O'Henry, who it must be said sounded more like a character from a *Carry On* film than a band. The Jugs period was short-lived, and he soon moved to the then-named Alan Bown Set, with whom he spent six years recording several albums. In 1975, he gave an interesting summary of his time between Alan Bown and Supertramp, stating:

I was with Alan Bown for about six years through all the ups and downs, and then after that, when it split up, I went and worked for a few strip clubs. No, hang on! The first job I got before that was working in a dry cleaning factory during the day and the Celebrity Club at night. Then, when I sorted out my tax problem, I left the dry cleaning job and the Celebrity Club and went on to play the Twilight Rooms where Doug was working, and then I got my big break … I joined Jimmy Johnson And The Bandwagon! Then I joined up with Arthur Conley and, later on, with Jimmy Ruffin. Each one was a step up. Then, I went to Germany and I came back in August to join this lot. They said they were making the album in September.

After the dissolution of the Alan Bown band, Dougie Thomson clearly took a mental note of John, as he recommended him for the Supertramp job. Looking back on the audition process in *Sounds*, Helliwell's comments are illuminating:

> I went home after playing with them and the wife asked me what it was like, and I said, 'Yeah, pretty good, but I think I'll go back tomorrow'. Then, I went the next day and came home and she said, 'Well, how do you feel about it now?' I said, 'It's alright, but I'll have to go again', and it kept on going like that. At the same time, I had to do a job during the day. So, I enlisted with Manpower and the first job I got was as a petrol pump attendant. Then, I got a job screwing nuts and bolts together at a factory in Maidenhead.

Nuts, bolts and petrol pumps aside, he clearly impressed the band enough, as he was hired – even though Roger Hodgson did state in 1983, 'We told John to keep his job at the gas station' (in other words, don't give up your day job just yet). This was, as much as anything, an indicator of the sense of uncertainty and financial risk which was still surrounding the band following the removal of their Sam-financed safety net. Therefore, this should not be interpreted as any sort of commentary on Helliwell's musical talents or suitability. Of course, despite this prudence, dispensing fuel was not required as a long-term option – and thus, the Crime Syndicate was permanently complete.

Concert setlists of the time are hard to come by, but the few BBC Radio sessions that the band did between 1972 and 1973 reveal several songs which never made it onto an album or, in some cases, onto vinyl in any form. The two sides of the non-album single 'Land Ho'/'Summer Romance' are generally known as having later turned up on the *Retrospectacle* compilation, but other songs aired during those sessions and never actually released commercially included 'Chicken Man', 'Down In Mexico', 'Laura', 'Pony Express' and 'Black Cat'. Reportedly, most, if not all, of these were making an appearance in shows of the time – in particular, the rocky 'Black Cat', which was very much a live regular. Songs which would make it onto *Crime Of The Century* were also beginning to be worked up and were being slotted into the set, albeit in rather rudimentary versions; 'Dreamer' and 'Bloody Well Right' were both included in a BBC Radio 1 session from March 1973, 'Dreamer' and 'Rudy' in November 1972 and

'School' and 'If Everyone Was Listening' even earlier in August 1972. Clearly, this was not going to be an album put together hastily.

The removal of Sam's financial support was naturally a hugely important blow to the band, though Davies has said that, in one way, it actually had a positive effect in that it forced them to focus their efforts and deliver the goods without a safety net allowing them to coast along at all. In a *New Musical Express* interview in 1975, Davies was honest about them having relied too much on Sam's support in the past:

There's no way you can't when you have somebody like that. It's like when you have a big record … well, this is the first experience we've had of any big sales, but already, signs of leaning on that are creeping in. It's something you've got to be careful of. A lot of musicians are really lazy and, speaking personally, you tend to grab any security that's going because you know what the business is like.

His recollection of the living arrangements when sharing a large communal house makes for even more eye-opening reading. He looked back on the time:

That was really bizarre when we had that house, the big house in Holland Villas. Joe Cocker was in there and there were only supposed to be four people to pay the rent, which was astronomical, so there were 12 of us in the end. There were people in the roof, all over the place. I was living in the shower. You should have seen the scene when the landlady came around to collect the rent. I've never seen anything like it. She came around about ten in the morning, and it was like 'panicsville'. The alarm went off, I got up and I walked straight out of the door with my pullover on; it was pouring with rain and I just walked round Shepherd's Bush. I didn't have money for breakfast or anything. I ended up bumming a quid off that guy at the Cabin. I expected everyone to be out in the street when I got back. I was surprised when everyone was still there. It was like a farce. People stark naked rushing from room to room as they were showing the landlady around; there were people hiding in the cupboards. They were going to check in the attic and, of course, there were tents in there!

Following a show in Manchester on 2 June 1973, the band took a break from live performances for almost exactly a year, with their next show coming on 31 May 1974 in Southend. With the band having weathered the difficult transitional period after the *Indelibly Stamped* album, the time had come to get the material into shape for what would become *Crime Of The Century*. Talking to me on the 40th anniversary of the album in 2014, Roger Hodgson did shed some light on that period and whether it was, in fact, something of a dark time:

Oh, that's certainly the case. It has been suggested that A&M might have put pressure on us to make the third album 'the one', but I never felt that, to be fair – they were always supportive. If there was a 'make or break' time, that was well before the recording, when the pressure was 'can we get to Manchester?', you know, 'have we got enough fuel to make the show?' … I must admit to wondering whether we had come to the end of the road – we were broke, we didn't have a band. I was actually having some ideas about trying other things, and I was planning to go to India, which was something I was really keen on at the time. Anyway, I still remember that we had a meeting one day, and we thought that we had some good songs up our sleeves – I had 'School' and 'Dreamer' and I knew he had 'Bloody Well Right' – and we thought, well let's just give it one more go. So, we lived partly by way of selling equipment for a while and we got some songs together and took them to A&M, and Jerry Moss, who is the M in A&M, of course, was very supportive, saying how good he thought the material was, and that we should definitely go for the album.

Without a doubt, the support of a helpful and positive record company was always a massive help during a tricky time for any artist – the stories down the years of labels effectively 'burying' albums which they didn't believe in, with no promotional budget, are depressingly common, as are examples of the original submission of the songs being rejected utterly with the demand to 'go away and write a hit'. In actual fact, there were a lot more songs 'in the bank' than the eight that would make up the final album, particularly from Hodgson's side. In addition to the aforementioned unrecorded pieces, the title track to the 1979 album *Breakfast In America* was already written (Roger again: 'In fact, it could have been on *Crime Of The Century*, but it definitely wouldn't have fit there! When it came to *Breakfast In America*, though, with the songs Rick had ready, it did fit), and there is at least one setlist from January 1975, on the *Crime* tour, which notes 'The Logical Song' as having been played. Roger explained to me in 2012 how his and Rick's writing differed when it came time for an album:

> For my part, I was always very prolific, and I always had a backlog of songs to choose from – I still do, to be honest. Rick, on the other hand, was the opposite – he would always come in with his five or six songs, so what I would do would be to dip into the collection of songs I had ready and see which of mine matched his – which was very much the case with the *Breakfast In America* album, for example.

With the album very much having been given the 'green light' by A&M and live work having been put on the back burner, the by-now settled band got down to the business of preparing the arrangements and finalising the songwriting for the record. To do this, they did what quite a lot of bands were doing in the early part of the 1970s – retreated to a private space to work. Roger again, in 2014:

> With the help of the record company, we were able to go away to a farm in the West Country to write, rehearse and generally get to know each other – we were following the old Traffic model of 'getting ourselves together in the country'! This period went really well, and we felt that as well as the stronger material, we had a band which was truly able to do them justice and sounded better than anything we'd had up to that point. When it came to the actual recording, we were pretty much focused on the eight songs which would make up the album – I had a backlog of songs myself, as I have always had, and we may have played through some of those, but when it came to putting the record together, we knew what it was going to be.

The farm in question was something of a bucolic surrounding, being a 17th-century building in Somerset. John Helliwell told *Sounds* in 1975:

> After the rehearsal studios in the Old Kent Road, we used to rehearse under Kew Bridge. Then we got together with A&M Records, who hired a cottage for us in Somerset; we managed to wangle a stay there. So, we all went there with girlfriends, wives, kids and cats. We were there for about three months.

Fully aware by now of the final shape which the finished album would take, the eight songs were worked on, having, in some cases, their arrangements thoroughly overhauled from their original onstage forms. The album was in a good state of planning by the time they came to begin recording in February 1974. The recording sessions went on until June, with the band determined to do this one right, and several London studios were used, including Trident, Scorpio Sound on Euston Road and The Who's Ramport Studios in Battersea. There was no chance of the band risking handling all of the production duties themselves this time out, and experienced producer/engineer Ken Scott was brought in. Scott knew his way around a recording studio, to say the least, having worked as an engineer for ten years since cutting his teeth as an assistant engineer with The Beatles, no less, and the *A Hard Day's Night* album. Going on to work in an engineering capacity on no less than seven Beatles albums, culminating in the *White Album* in 1968, he also numbered the likes of Jeff Beck, Van der Graaf Generator and Procol Harum among his clients, progressing to the producer's chair with David Bowie for *Hunky Dory* in 1971. He went on to produce both *Ziggy Stardust* and *Aladdin Sane* for Bowie, as well as a couple of albums by jazz-rock drummer Billy Cobham. He seemed to have all of the credentials to be a perfect fit to produce the album alongside the Supertramp members themselves, and so it proved. One of the notable triumphs regularly acknowledged about the *Crime Of The Century* album has always been its superlative sound quality, something which was very important given the intricately balanced and finessed nature of the material.

The Album And The Songs

Personnel:
Rick Davies: vocals, keyboards, harmonica
Roger Hodgson: vocals, guitar, piano
John Helliwell: saxophone, clarinet, backing vocals
Dougie Thomson: bass
Bob C. Benberg: drums, percussion
Produced by Ken Scott and Supertramp
String arrangements by Richard Hewson
Record Label: A&M
Recorded: February-June 1974
Release date: 13 September 1974
Highest chart places: UK: 4; US: 38
Running time: 44:10
All tracks are credited as written by Hodgson and Davies

Right away, the thorny question of the conceptual nature of the album must be addressed. The band have always denied that it was written as any sort of concept (with one notable exception) but rather that any sort of thematic link was a fortuitous one, which emerged when they arranged the tracks to best fit the running order after the recording was complete. Many people believe this to be either untrue or, at the very least, some obfuscation of the facts to fit the narrative they preferred to present. This must be countered by the question of why they would wish to deny that conceptual nature and what they might have gained from it, given that the stock of the concept album with the rock audience was at something of an all-time high in 1974, not least because of the astonishing reach and influence of Pink Floyd's *Dark Side Of The Moon* the previous year.

Speaking to me in 2012, in fact, and asked about the individual character arc running through the first six songs at least, Roger's reflections about the conceptual nature or otherwise were quite illuminating:

Well, it certainly was a magical time, that's for sure, and we had all the time in the world to come up with the goods, which I think we did. The concept thing wasn't as overt as you suggest, though. We did certainly start off with the intention of writing a concept album, but that only really got as far as the first couple of tracks. I wrote 'School' and then Rick modified 'Bloody Well Right' to fit with that, with the 'So you think your schooling's phoney' line, but after that, it just became more a case of arranging the songs we'd written to see what would work best in what order because we always wrote separately, of course. It's great that you can see a theme running through it like that, whereas, for Rick and myself, it was more a case of us putting ourselves on our sleeves if you like and laying out elements of ourselves in our songs. 'Hide In Your Shell', for example, very much reflected me at that time, as I did tend to hide in my shell to protect myself from the world in a way, and similarly, 'Asylum' had some relevance to Rick at that time as he definitely had some inner demons going on. 'Dreamer', again, was me being very much a dreamer back then, so if there is a concept, it's probably more along those lines of our own personalities. Your interpretation is interesting, though – and it probably shows how you have the benefit of distance and perspective, whereas I was too close to it.

So, from that, an almost 'unconscious concept' due to their own personalities, strengthened by the song placement, seems about as far as it might have gotten in terms of any intent.

That said, the link between the majority of the songs on the album seems an extremely strong one. So, for the purposes of this discussion, I will look at the conceptual links between the themes and leave it up to the individual to decide what extent this might have been deliberately planned or, conversely, an unconscious linking of the material which only fully revealed itself when the pieces were put together.

'School' (5:35)

Roger Hodgson takes the lead vocal, as it is primarily his work (this pattern is followed throughout the album and, indeed, the band's career from this point).

The track opens with the somewhat incongruous sound of a wistful harmonica played by Rick Davies. 'Incongruous' not only in that it's not the instrument you expect to hear in this particular genre, but also not one employed very often by the band (generally one track per album, if that) – and yet, it opens the first track, front and centre. That said, it's very effective, seeming to arrest the listener's attention and make them listen in the manner that a school bell would function to signal to the pupils. This is a good example of the sort of small details which make this album, and indeed most Supertramp records, so precise. It's a little like the Steely Dan method of planning everything down to the smallest degree yet still making it appear uncluttered and spontaneous – it's a clever trick for sure.

The harmonica continues for around 45 seconds, being subtly joined by other instrumentation after about 20 seconds before Roger Hodgson comes in, accompanying himself on guitar as he sings the opening lines:

I can see you in the morning on your way to school
Don't forget your books, you know you've got to learn the Golden Rule

This is a nice, concise way to introduce the main protagonist around whom the concept – if indeed there is one – revolves, here starting his journey through life as a schoolboy.

It is interesting at this point to note the use of 'the Golden Rule', which has been used in songs about education ever since Chuck Berry noted it being taught in the song 'School Days', without much in the way of context about what it is exactly. The general consensus, when searching through the writings of those who chronicle such things, is that the 'Golden Rule' refers to the fundamental moral principle of treating others as you would have them treat you in return, which was put forth in the Gospel of St Mark as 'Do as you would be done by'. This is certainly a sound principle around which to base one's life choices, I'm sure most would agree – but it is hard to see how remembering one's school books would be necessary to grasp it. In any case, the jungle-like environment of the typical schoolyard and classroom would be the last place for such advice to be followed (at least in my own experience!). One might well surmise that the 'Golden Rule' referred to in this and other school-based songs would more properly apply to any policy which a given teacher propounds as vital at any particular time. Life and school, after all, are shifting platforms of such ever-changing social niceties.

Anyhow, leaving that particular sociological discussion aside for the moment, the following couplet has a greater significance in terms of the album as a whole:

Teacher tells you stop your play and get on with your work
And be like Johnny-too-good, well don't you know he never shirks
He's coming along

The generically identified 'Johnny-too-good' here, in his position as the protagonist's nemesis – with whom he is encouraged to try to keep up – foreshadows the character of 'Jimmy Cream', who provides much the same function in the song 'Asylum'. These can be seen as an illustration, metaphorical if you will, of the impossible expectations with which we are all burdened throughout life – 'keeping up with the Joneses' (or the 'too-goods' or the 'Creams').

Following the cap on the end of the verse with 'He's coming along' – further emphasising the irritatingly positive qualities of Johnny – there follows a short section with some slightly processed guitar repeating the simple opening phrase of the song in a slightly abstract fashion, as children's playground voices are interspersed. It is worth noting the skill involved in placing this almost ambient section so early in the opening song before the album has even built up a head of steam, yet still making the track seem like a very memorable and catchy one, which again, demonstrates the enormously clever and accomplished nature of the composition and playing here. Incidentally, the recording of the children was made by producer Ken Scott and, notably, features the sound of a particular girl's voice letting out a scream, which could be of laughter or otherwise, just as the whole band come in and the song 'proper' begins. In an interview with *Acoustic Storm* in 2010, Roger Hodgson was asked whether that scream does indeed intentionally project a double meaning of innocent laughter or the dread of the school experience lying ahead, and his reply was interesting:

> Yes. Nothing is accidental. I mean, when I arrange my songs, nothing is by accident. Everything, especially that scream that you're talking about just before the band come in, does represent a lot, so what you're feeling is right. I mean, you know, school is a wonderful place. Obviously, it's a school playground but that scream does represent a lot more.

Interestingly, the sound of the schoolchildren is an entirely natural one, as Ken Scott took a tape recorder with him to his daughter's school and simply recorded the cauldron of noise generated by the children coming out at the end of the day.

As soon as the full band enter, it's straight into the second verse, delivered more forcefully than the first, in a brilliantly effective injection of urgency. The protagonist is now playing in the park after the school day, being advised not to stay too late or after dark, which is all sage and well-intentioned advice, of course. However, then comes the first hint that learning that rule and keeping up with Johnny is not so simple, as an agenda to keep the individual in their place is suggested:

They tell you not to hang around and learn what life's about
And grow up just like them, won't you let it work it out
And you're full of doubt

Immediately, the tone of the song has shifted from the calm inference of everything being okay if we behave ourselves and strive for scholastic excellence (echoed by the restrained accompaniment) to the much more urgent warning that it is, in fact, a big, bad world out there and seemingly protective people want to keep you in line (again, echoed by the more strident music, and indeed, by that scream).

The music then takes another turn into the sort of almost ambient, reflective mood which comes directly after the first verse, letting the song drift along for a while in this pensive manner, with subdued yet effective guitar fills taking the weight. Suddenly, an insistent drumbeat heralds a change of pace as things burst into a brilliantly effective piano-led instrumental section, with Rick Davies excelling (notably, though this is Hodgson's song in the main, Davies wrote this piano mid-section), and the two elements dovetail masterfully.

A sudden shift into a heavy middle-eight, with a far more aggressive feel to it, reinforces the already-implied reality of societal coercion strongly, opening with the stern words, 'Don't do this, and don't do that', and ending with the unequivocal manipulative threat of:

Don't criticise, they're old and wise
Do as they tell you to
Don't want the devil to
Come out and put your eyes

Hodgson and Davies trade vocal lines in this part of the song, and things have clearly taken a darker and more serious turn, with a brief guitar-led instrumental bridge taking us from this into an abrupt return to the verse section, with a funkier edge and even more aggression, as the narrator of the song lays bare his despair and frustration with, 'Maybe I'm mistaken expecting you to fight...', before ending the verse, and the lyric, with:

But while I am still living, I've just got this to say
It's always up to you if you want to be that
Want to see that, want to see that way
You're coming along

The use of 'You're coming along' to end things here is deliberate and telling, as it calls back to Johnny-too-good in the first verse, who is also 'coming along', but here implying that to truly better yourself and progress (and find yourself 'coming along'), life, rather than the classroom, will be the battleground. A final crescendo, with a subtle musical callback to the mid-song instrumental section, closes an opener which crucially sets the scene for the album and manages to say far more than one would expect from its relatively concise lyric.

We are now at the section of the album which even the band admit was deliberately written as a conceptual whole, as the next track enters …

'Bloody Well Right' (4:32)

The opening of this song of Rick's is deceptive – lasting only four and a half minutes (one of only three sub-five minute tracks on the album), the first 50 seconds or so are taken up by a lazy, jazzy electric piano introduction – almost unaccompanied, though punctuated by occasional urgent chordal stabs as if interjecting to hurry things along. At this point, it morphs into a more progressive-flavoured full-band passage, led by some guitar work with a slightly funky edge and liberally doused in wah-wah. This continues for roughly that same 50 seconds again before, just as one could be forgiven for wondering whether it might be an instrumental track – as we are a third of the way through – it takes a sharp left turn into what is essentially a heavy metal riff ushering in the angrily-delivered verse:

> So you think your schooling is phoney,
> I guess it's hard not to agree
> You say it all depends on money
> And who is in your family tree.

As we have seen, this is the only part of the album which the band admitted was deliberately planned in a conceptual way, with the link from the powerlessness of the pupils in 'School' to this pent-up rant of frustration.

After the grinding riff (and interjections of lead guitar licks) which powers the verse, the song takes its most startling change yet, with the chorus line of 'Right, you're bloody well right, you got a bloody right to say' delivered against a suddenly staccato and sparse electric piano. There is a reason for this change of approach, however, as it highlights the change in approach of the narrator, from seemingly angry to sarcastically dismissive. Following several reiterations of how 'bloody well right' the complainant is and what a valid right he has to raise the issue, the chorus ends with the key line, 'Me I don't care anyway...'. This would appear to be the voice of the 'establishment' mocking and disregarding these perceived injustices, something reiterated by the second verse, delivered again over the aggressive riffing and in a far more threatening manner:

Write your problems down in detail
Take them to a higher place
You've had your cry – no, I should say wail
In the meantime hush your face.

This is a crushingly dismissive blow to the complainant, as the narrator of the verses, as well as the chorus, is revealed as the same voice representing the system, the establishment, the 'order', or however you wish to phrase it. With bitingly aggressive sarcasm, he urges the object of his withering scorn to make out his complaints in a full and accurate manner and raise them with the proper authorities before sneering that this will be futile as he is, in essence, an irrelevance to the way the world works. It's a contemptuously patronising way of patting the person on the head and saying, 'There, there, you have your little tantrum and then get over it' – and there must surely have been millions of listeners (and still must be today) who have experienced this exact same feeling of powerlessness in the face of an uncaring system. If Pink Floyd kind of rephrased 'School' in 'Another Brick In The Wall', this one is essentially saying 'Welcome To The Machine' – a universal issue dealt with in different ways.

It would be remiss to pass this second verse by without giving mention to the dreadfully clumsy rhyme of 'no, I should say wail' with 'write your problems down in detail', but it gets something of a pass considering the concise way the song delivers its message. The eight verse lines and the choruses, which are mostly repetitions of 'you're bloody well right' and 'you got a bloody well right to say', are punctured spectacularly by the 'me I don't care anyway' pay-off, which is delivered just the once at the end of the first chorus (it isn't needed again, the effect has been produced). After the second and final chorus, the song heads toward a fade, with Davies vamping on the 'got a bloody right to say' theme over John Helliwell's jazzy saxophone coda. The song has been through jazz, heavy metal, prog rock, funk and pop over the course of four and a half minutes, which indicates just how Supertramp had quickly developed the knack of making complexities sound simple.

It is worth noting that Rick Davies was the only person who could sing this song. Obviously, he would have done anyhow, as he and Hodgson each take lead vocals on the songs which were wholly or mainly written by them (four apiece), but Hodgson's more reedy and almost fragile vocal tones could not have carried the sneering aggression of this song in the same way as Davies, whose voice is more powerful, if perhaps not as melodic. A clear example of opposites melding to form a greater whole.

The song was released as the B-side to the 'Dreamer' single, but interestingly, in the US, it was strongly preferred to its nominal A-side and went on to be the featured cut on the single, reaching number 35 in the *Billboard* chart – an unusual case of a band's breakthrough hit in a particular country never having technically been released as a single there.

'Hide In Your Shell' (6:49)

Written entirely by Roger Hodgson, 'Hide In Your Shell' is not only a key song on the album but is one of Roger's most personal songs, dealing with some of the issues he faced. As he told me in 2014:

At the time, I was very much yearning to find some meaning for a lot of things in my life, and a relationship with God and my spiritual side. I turned vegetarian at the time, and I was reading a lot of books which had a profound effect on shaping my personality and outlook on life. The rest of the band didn't really share most of my ideas – indeed, quite the opposite, as I did face quite a bit of ridicule in the ensuing years – so that song was really very much about me, spending quite a lot of time hiding in my own shell and wanting to break out. It's interesting, I think, that both Rick and I did the same thing on that album, wearing our hearts on our sleeves as it were, and that probably is a large part of the reason why it resonates with people so much.

In the context of the album concept – assuming, of course, that there is one – the song appears to reflect the protagonist realising how the odds are stacked against him in life and retreating into himself, or his 'shell', to gain some perceived protection from the world at large. This time, there is no prolonged prologue, just a small dual-keyboard introductory passage before Roger comes in, his more fragile voice

Above: The iconic and evocative *Crime Of The Century* front cover. (*A&M*)

Below: The rear cover featuring the oddly unclothed band. (*A&M*)

Above: Supertramp in July 1974. Left to right: John Helliwell, Dougie Thomson, Bob Siebenberg, Roger Hodgson, Rick Davies. (*Michael Ochs Archives/Getty Images*)

Below: Roger and Rick – with a can of Double Diamond dating the photograph! (*Fin Costello/Redferns*)

Above: A rather striking billboard on Sunset Strip, Los Angeles, in 1974. Welcome to America, indeed. (*Alamy*)

Below: A press kit photo showing the band at the piano in what we suspect might just be a posed shot. (*A&M*)

Supertramp

L to R: RICK DAVIES, DOUGIE THOMSON,
JOHN A. HELLIWELL, ROGER HODGSON, BOB C. BENBERG

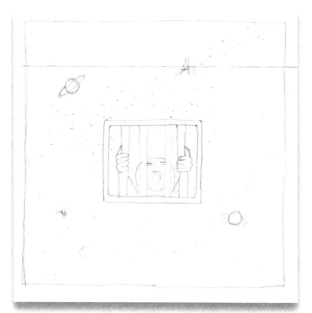

Above: An artist's work-in-progress sketch for the cover. (*by kind permission of Paul Wakefield*)

Below: A second work-in-progress sketch showing more recognisable development. (*by kind permission of Paul Wakefield*)

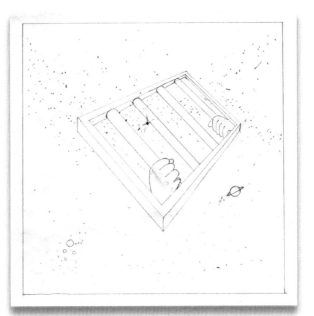

Above: A final sketch showing the design coming together, though still depicting Saturn at this time. (*by kind permission of Paul Wakefield*)

Below: A single of the track 'School', released belatedly in the Netherlands in 1983 and backed with 'Oh Darling' from *Breakfast In America*, somewhat randomly. (*A&M*)

Above: Roger Hodgson in a *Midnight Special* TV performance of 'Hide In Your Shell' in 1975.

Below: Rick Davies in that same *Midnight Special* appearance.

Above: John Helliwell and Dougie Thomson in the 1975 'Hide In Your Shell' TV performance.

Below: A fourth shot from the *Midnight Special* appearance, this time with Bob behind the drum kit.

Above: A 1975 Yugoslavian release of 'Dreamer', backed as usual with 'Bloody Well Right', on the Jugoton label. (*A&M*)

Below: 'Bloody Well Right' was famously used as the A-side to 'Dreamer' in the US, but this one is from the Netherlands, 1975, and backed with 'If Everyone Was Listening'. (*A&M*)

perfectly embodying the vulnerability and anxiety so prominent in the lyrics. The stall is set out immediately as he begins:

Hide in your shell, 'cause the world is out to bleed you for a ride
What will you gain making your life a little longer?

Serious stuff indeed, and it goes on to reflect on the reasons which have driven him to this most uncomfortable and defensive of positions:

Heaven or hell, was the journey cold that gave you eyes of steel?
Shelter behind, painting your mind and playing joker

The question 'was the journey cold that gave you eyes of steel?' resonates very strongly. Of course, it reflects on the unfairness and difficulties which have served to make the character so bitter and mistrusting of people and situations, but it seems to be also subtly emphasising the phrase 'cold steel', which only reinforces the image conjured up by the line. 'Playing joker' is clearly taken from Roger's own experiences of having to take cruel remarks and laugh them off, or at least present a façade of doing so, while 'painting your mind' is a nice metaphor for retreating into an inner world of fantastical constructs in order to help erect the wall against the outside world (once again, Roger Waters wasn't the first to this particular subject...).

At this point, the music becomes a little more urgent, with just an undercurrent of menace, as Roger details some of the issues faced by himself/the protagonist (depending on whether we are looking at the song as a confessional or a conceptual piece). It's clear that his withdrawal has left him with significant social difficulties:

Too frightening to listen to a stranger
Too beautiful to put your pride in danger
You're waiting for someone to understand you

It is notable that the 'too frightening' and 'too beautiful' phrases are delivered by a choir of backing vocals as if this is something being drummed into the subject by either his own subconscious or the world around him. It certainly seems to herald a darker mood as the drums suddenly enter here, as this bridging section, or pre-chorus if you like, takes on a more insistent tone, with the next lines having a call-and-response technique (with Davies, from the sound of it) repeating and emphasising the urgency of them:

You've got demons in your closet (you got demons in your closet)
And you're screaming out to stop it (and you're screaming out to stop it)
Saying life's begun to cheat you, Friends are out to beat you
Grab on to what you can scramble for.

This is clearly culminating in a sort of 'if you can't beat them, join them' feeling, as this sensitive soul is being encouraged to give up trying to be different, or to rise above his threatening surroundings, and to become just as dog-eat-dog himself in an attempt to fit in. As if to refute the need for this surrender of principle and dignity, a conciliatory voice of support, as if from someone who understands the situation and has experienced it, arrives immediately to cut off those baser instincts in their tracks and offer a much-needed hand:

Don't let the tears linger on inside now
Because it's sure time you gained control
If I can help you, if I can help you
If I can help you, just let me know
Well, let me show you the nearest signpost
To get your heart back and on the road
If I can help you, if I can help you
If I can help you, just let me know.

This chorus, awash with swirling keyboards, as well as some brilliantly sympathetic saxophone from John Helliwell, is the most uplifting part of the song – and arguably of the whole album – and each time it is repeated, it becomes even more so. Even today, Roger insists that he gets people telling him regularly how much this song has helped them personally through dark periods of their lives. As he told me in 2014:

That is the most requested song that I get, but it isn't just people asking to hear it; it's the way they tell me, when they ask for it, how much it has meant to them as individuals in their lives, which really touches me very deeply as a songwriter. I shared my pain and my frustration in the song, and the way it has come back to me in terms of touching other people around the world is something that is an incredible feeling.

Coming down from the chorus via a return to the understated keyboards of the song intro, along with some subtle touches of backing vocal, the song continues to detail the anxieties and insecurities being felt by the subject:

All through the night as you lie awake and hold yourself so tight
What do you need, a second hand movie star to tend you

The clear implication here is that no amount of hero-worship of idols or other 'pin-ups' will help. Roger, in his role as the support mechanism of sorts, continues to lay his own experience out still more plainly as he redoubles his empathetic message:

I as a boy, I believed the saying the cure for pain was love
How would it be if you could see the world through my eyes

This further continues as we go into the pre-chorus again, with the first three lines now:

Too frightening – the fire's becoming colder
Too beautiful – to think you're getting older
You're now looking for someone to give an answer

This shows that help is being more urgently requested, and things are perhaps coming to something of a head, with the following 'friends are out to beat you' feelings now preceded by: 'What you see is just illusion/You're surrounded by confusion'. This is a very troubled individual, but once again, that soothing voice and calming instrumental accompaniment of the chorus enters like a balm applied to a wound.

Following the next chorus, there is something of a mid-section, wherein Roger's vocal becomes ever more supportive and longing to help, urgently repeating the mantras of 'Why do you hold yourself down?', 'Never ever let yourself go', and then, 'There's a place I know the way to, a place there is no need to feel you're all alone'.

As the music continues to wrap itself around the words like a supporting blanket of sound, he assures the sufferer that 'I know exactly what you're feeling, Cause all your troubles are within you' in a way which leaves the listener in no doubt of his empathy and sincerity. Finally, the song comes towards its end as he urges:

Love me, love you
Loving is the way to
Help me, help you

At this point, the music and the insistent backing vocals repeating the supportive message continue to spiral ever upward, and the effect is quite remarkable. Roger himself emphasised to me how he wanted the tension and release of the song from a musical perspective to work:

> Yes, that's exactly what I was trying to do with that. It was intended to massage your heart and soul as it ebbs and flows, with a big cathartic release at the end. It's marvellous to hear people saying it works so well because we took so much care and attention when recording the little details, the vocal harmonies and everything. There's even a musical saw in the chorus, which my band now use to reproduce it onstage!

There is a slight twist, however, as the lyric finally takes a turn to a regretful tone, addressing the sad fact that, all too often, people will not open up to allow themselves to be helped with the rueful lines:

> Why must we be so cool, oh so cool
> Oh, we're such damn fools

That final line fades out so as to be barely audible as the band play out with that continuing inspirational chorus melody, with backing vocals still repeating promises of help. What are we to assume from this? That we must go on trying to help even if it is all too often futile? Or that, perhaps, love and support can overcome the resistance to accept that help? Whether it is an upbeat or downbeat ending is up to the listener to decide. Whatever the truth of it, the overall effect of the song, as attested to by so many people over the years, is nothing less than a masterclass in self-help.

Roger must have the final word here, as he spoke to me in 2014 about how the song was still touching people's lives:

> In some ways, I haven't spoken as much as I would like about the song, but it's something that I really want to express. Just recently, for example, there was a comment on the guestbook on my website from an 18-year-old girl – I must stress that some of the things people write on that guestbook are incredible and very important to me. Anyway, this particular girl wrote a comment saying that if it hadn't been for that song, she wouldn't be alive today, but that she was now going through her Final exams, which is something that

touches you in a way that no amount of record sales or anything like that can match. I never could have realised at the time of writing the song – struggling to get out of my own shell and gain the courage to face the world – that it would have helped so many other people for so long. Incredible, really.

And if that doesn't sum up the brilliance of the song more than any review ever could, I don't know what I could do to emphasise it further.

One interesting point to mention is that of the backing vocalists on the track. One of these was Christine Helliwell (John's wife), with another being Bob Benberg's wife Vicky Siebenberg. The third is more unexpected, being none other than Scott Gorham, guitarist with Thin Lizzy and most definitely not known as a singer! The reason for his appearance is that Vicky was his sister, making him Bob's brother-in-law when the pair married in 1974 – both men came over to the UK to pursue their musical careers (Gorham following two years after Benberg in 1973, hoping the two could play together, which did not come to pass). Bob became the only American in Supertramp, with Scott coincidentally later finding himself in the same position with Thin Lizzy.

'Asylum' (6:44)

Closing the first side of the original vinyl, Rick Davies' 'Asylum' advances things as our unfortunate hero retreats further into his own mental issues – possibly having failed to get help owing to the 'We're such damn fools' payoff at the end of 'Hide In Your Shell'. He is bullish about his own sanity while simultaneously revealing the problems he has with his state of mind, almost contradicting himself in his bravado in places. Right at the beginning of the song, we meet another nemesis, Jimmy Cream, who is always better off and more stable than he is – this could perhaps be the same 'Johnny-too-good' who is the similarly envied over-achiever in 'School', or it may simply be another in a long line of people next to whom he feels inferior and somewhat defensive. This is laid out plainly in the opening lines:

Jimmy Cream was keen, his brain was always winning
I can't keep tabs on mine – it's really quite a joke
I see him down the road, I ask if he'd be willing
To lend me 15p, I'm dying for a smoke

It is interesting to note how the '15p for a smoke' line has failed to age well, as presumably, this would have bought a packet of cigarettes in 1974: in 2024, 15p would get you slightly less than a quarter of a single cigarette, which wouldn't be a lot of help when 'dying for a smoke'!

The track begins with a plaintive, wistful piano theme, which seems to evoke a certain vagueness, indicative of the individual who is just failing to 'keep tabs' on his thoughts. This continues behind the first verse until, on the word 'smoke', it spirals to a higher note (as does the smoke from a cigarette). It could also indicate the high of a different type of 'smoke', but even in 1974, one would imagine requiring a little more than 15p to avail oneself of that herbal accessory. Even at this early stage of the song, the main character is becoming a little defensive, with the chorus seeing him demanding:

Don't arrange to have me sent to no asylum
I'm just as sane as anyone
It's just a game I play for fun

He re-emphasises this in the short second verse ...

. I told 'em 'Look!', I said 'I'm not the way you're thinkin'
. Just when I'm down, I'll be the clown, I'll play the fool'

...before returning to the plea not to be sent to an asylum in the chorus again. This may fall on deaf ears, however, as the following section of the song hints that he may indeed have ended up in such an institution. It is after this second chorus that the band come in, teasing with a gradual build until all come in together for the triumphant-sounding vocals – which are far from triumphant for the subject but may be deliberately seen as that from the point of view of the staff of the asylum. The first potential clue as to where he has ended up may come in the first few lines of this part:

Will he take a sailboat ride?
Well he is very likely to
Will he feel good inside?
Well he ain't very likely to

This could be a reference to the book *One Flew Over The Cuckoo's Nest* (the film had yet to be made), in which the inmate does, in fact, go on a fishing trip. Of course, 'taking a sailboat ride' could simply be a metaphor for him having a mental health episode. Whatever the truth of it, the following lines confirm him as being non-communicative:

Will he tell you he's alive?
Yeah he is always trying to
But nothin', no, no nothin', does he say
In the morning when the day's begun
'Hello Good morning, how are you?'
And in the evening or the noonday sun
'What a lovely afternoon'
Well I've been living next to you

Roger Hodgson delivers the 'Good morning' and 'Lovely afternoon' lines, demonstrating that they are spoken by someone else attempting to get the subject to respond. The final 'Well I've been living next to you' could be a fellow inmate, or it could be a staff member. Either way, it seems that he is now in the very asylum that he wanted so badly to avoid. This is laid out even more starkly in the next verse, as the music drops to the piano-led verse accompaniment again, only this time, with fuller instrumentation and woozy-sounding string interjections – it is clearly the inmate in the first person speaking this time:

Bluesy Monday is the one day that they come here
Yeah when they haunt me and they taunt me in my cage
I mock them all, they're feeling small, they got no answer
Yeah they're playin' dumb, but I'm just laughing as they rage

This is followed up by a further seemingly baseless plea not to be sent to an asylum again when he is clearly being treated by doctors whom he taunts with uncooperative responses. The chorus, this time, ends with the extra line, 'Yeah, I've been trying to fool everyone'. The paradox here is that if he is indeed sane and is just putting on his crazy act to fool the doctors, then he is only hurting himself by convincing them that he is mad, which cannot be the action of a sane individual.

The music starts to swell again here, with Davies seemingly randomly mumbling, 'Are you ready? No that's too heavy', before the 'Sailboat Ride' section comes in again with an even more dramatic sweep than before. This time, however, things change when we get to Roger being the person talking to him again, as he now seems to be replying but without much apparent sense:

In the morning when the day's begun
'Do you think it looks like rain?'
And in the evening or the noonday sun
'You know I nearly missed my train'

Of course, if Roger voicing these lines indicates the subject himself speaking, then it could correlate that he was delivering the corresponding 'Hello good morning how are you' lines, though he is shown to be non-communicative at that time, so a logical unravelling of the lines becomes – perhaps intentionally – difficult to rationalise. Whichever one of them is speaking now goes on to say:

Well I've been living next to you my friend
But what kind of friend are you?

These lines are clearly up for interpretation, but the following few lines, as we get towards the end of the song, seem to indicate that his attempt at playing crazy while being either sane or thinking himself to be sane is not going to end well:

Oh, is it the beginning or the sorry end?
Will I ever see it through?
No I've never been insane
Oh what's the game?
I believe I'm dying!

This is followed by the climactic section of the song, with squalling lead guitar and muted horns sounding like demented laughter before real demented laughter enters along with the crazed line, 'He's mad mad mad mad mad!', followed by a cry of 'Not quite right!' (as opposed to previously being 'quite right, bloody well right', perhaps). The crescendo suddenly drops off again to the opening piano theme, which gradually fades out to nothing.

Note that if you listen closely, after the fade-out, a single cry of a cuckoo can barely be heard. Is this another reference to *One Flew Over The Cuckoo's Nest*, or simply a light-hearted reference to the character being 'cuckoo'? Either way, it's a neat full-stop to the song, which ends the first side of the original vinyl on a big, dramatic and dark note to counterbalance the uplifting mood of 'Hide In Your Shell'. It is this yin and yang between the Hodgson and Davies songs which makes this album so much more than the sum of its parts and leads to its exceptional replay value. What can be around the corner on side two for our hero, however?

'Dreamer' (3:31)

The shortest song on the album, Hodgson's 'Dreamer' has ended up being the signature song on the album, the band's first hit single (except in the US, where it was flipped over for 'Bloody Well Right' to be the hit) and one of the most recognised Supertramp songs of all. As Hodgson put it to *Record Mirror* in 1975:

> When the album came out, we had no thoughts of a single, but we knew that if there was going to be a single, then 'Dreamer' would be it. It was simply the most commercial track on the album. We couldn't go out and pen a single. We don't write like that.

In fact, the song 'Dreamer' was, so Roger had claimed, written in his mother's house years before when he was just 19 years old, the first time he had the opportunity to play a Wurlitzer piano. However, like so many songs over the course of the Supertramp catalogue, it waited in the wings until the right time came to use it; its inclusion on *Crime* proved to be perfect timing, not only in terms of its success and what it meant to the band but also the seamless way in which it fitted into the narrative arc of the album. The instruments John Helliwell has been credited with contributing to the track are surely among the more unusual ones to appear on a rock song, as he is noted firstly as playing the celeste, or 'bell piano', which is a sort of piano-percussion hybrid, most famously heard in Tchaikovsky's 'Dance Of The Sugar Plum Fairy' from *The Nutcracker*. Even more unexpectedly, he has also been credited with playing the 'glass harp', which is an instrument bizarrely made up of upright wine glasses. In fact, in an appearance on *The Old Grey Whistle Test* in 1974, Helliwell can be seen playing the rim of a wine glass during a performance of the track. These instruments are not, in fact, noted in the album credits – which are somewhat sparse – but are documented in various internet references.

The whole song is based around a catchy and repetitive electric piano figure which opens the song, Hodgson accompanying himself for the first verse and chorus before the rest of the band enter in what is an effortlessly subtle and well-planned arrangement. With the first verse, Hodgson introduces the 'dreamer' of the title, illustrating how his dreams cannot be made reality and are ultimately self-defeating if relied upon too much. To put this idea across, he uses the metaphor of the dreamer trying to put his hands into his own head and touch the dream, making it a reality:

Dreamer, you know you are a dreamer
Well can you put your hands in your head, oh no!

It's a simple and memorable image and one which is soon skilfully referenced again. For now, there is what could be described as the first 'chorus' (though the song structure is rather nebulous in that way):

I said 'Far out, what a day, a year, a life it is!'
You know, well you know, you had it comin' to you
Now, there's not a lot I can do

This is immediately followed by the admonishment, harking back to the first lines:

Dreamer, you stupid little dreamer
So now you put your head in your hands, oh no!

This is very artfully deployed, demonstrating at a stroke how the dreamer, having failed to be able to 'put his hands in his head', is left forced to 'put his head in his hands' and regret his tapestry of fantasy. This also appears to be echoed by the 'Far out, what a day, a year, a life it is' line, perhaps being the dreamer rejoicing in his own train of ultimately pointless thought. Furthermore, the head-shaking comment of 'you know you had it coming to you, now there's not a lot I can do' indicates attempts to help him which have failed – possibly, of course, leading to him being admitted to an asylum, but certainly having harmed himself with his self-delusions.

The music in this section begins to build. First, Davies joins on keyboards, and then, as the 'now you put your head in your hands' line ends the short second verse, the band enter with a whoop from Hodgson, going into a rather funky groove thanks in no small measure to Dougie Thomson's bass, all still based around that same electric piano signature, but much changed in mood. One of the most simple yet impressive pieces of arrangement here is the phased and echoed vocals on the 'Far out!' exclamation, which lifts the line considerably and delivers a memorable hook right there and then. Once again, the care and attention to each small detail in the arrangements of the songs contribute enormously to the impact of the songs themselves and provide much of the genuinely 'progressive' nature of the music here.

After a short instrumental section and a fuller arrangement of the 'Far out!' chorus again, the music drops down to a more reflective, almost jazzy interlude, building up slowly via another very effective call-and-response vocal section between Davies and Hodgson, with the clearly insecure 'dreamer' being encouraged and assured of his own potential:

(If I could see something) – you can see anything you want, boy
(If I could be someone) – you can be anyone, celebrate, boy
(If I can do something) – you can do something
(If I could do anything) – but can you do something out of this world?

The music now inexorably begins to build, with the bass and drums increasing in intensity behind the piano as he is urged:

Take a dream on a Sunday
Take a life, take a holiday
Take a lie, take a dreamer

This last line is an odd one and can be interpreted in different ways. The 'take a lie' could mean accepting that the 'dream' is ultimately just that, or indeed, all three lines could be the dreamer himself insisting on how good and pleasant things are within his own fantasy world. In any case, the music bursts forth, now with a joyous-sounding ensemble passage accompanying a section filled with calls to 'Dream, dream, dream, dream along'.

The song comes to its climax here, with the 'dream along' refrain acting as counterpoint accompaniment to Roger's frantic reprise of the 'Dreamer, you know you are a dreamer' lines again until it all comes to a head with a final:

But can you put your head in your hands, oh no
Oh no
Oh no!

At which point, the music abruptly stops dead, replaced only with the gradually fading sounds of a musical box as if used by a child. The inference is clear: the dreamer has returned to his safe place within his own head and is lost to his would-be helpers. It's a dark and downbeat conclusion, but absolutely in keeping with the rest of the songs on the album. It's a fairly safe bet that, owing to the 'feelgood' effect of the musical arrangement, few listeners of the single will have picked up on any apparently dark undertone, in much the same way as so many casual listeners missed the entire message of Bruce Springsteen's hyper-critical 'Born In The USA', or took the bricks in the wall in Pink Floyd's 'Another Brick In The Wall' to be the students, unaware of the actual concept of the character 'Pink' and his own mental wall. Still, like those two songs, it remains a truly great single, so perhaps, ultimately, the message can be whatever you perceive or want it to be.

In terms of the album concept (as we are treating it), it is clear, however, that there are still significant challenges to overcome for the central character here, who may, indeed, finally be named in the next song...

'Rudy' (7:20)

The longest track on the album, and arguably the most complex in terms of the amount of different themes and musical twists and turns it incorporates, the clear inference from 'Rudy' is that it is the name of the character described throughout. It certainly appears to outline the somewhat nebulous fate of the unfortunate individual as a consequence of the numerous issues piled on his shoulders up to this point.

The song opens with a sparse, jazzy piano (not electric but a traditional acoustic piano this time), which meanders along until it coalesces into the first verse at the 40-second mark when Davies comes in with an immediately stark assessment of affairs:

Rudy's on a train to nowhere, halfway down the line
He don't wanna get there, but he needs time.
He ain't sophisticated, or well educated
After all the hours he's wasted, still he needs time

This is a fairly damning indictment of Rudy's life and his journey to this point. Clearly going nowhere in his life, he is self-aware enough to know that he doesn't want this path to continue, but as on a railway track, he is powerless to change it. We are told that he is not sophisticated or 'well educated', showing that he did indeed fritter away any opportunities he had in 'School'. Moreover, the biting line, 'after all the hours he's wasted, still he needs time', lays the blame squarely at his own door, as he frittered away time (and the opportunity to better himself), which he now needs when it is too late. You sense immediately that things are unlikely to take a positive turn for Rudy any time soon, and sure enough, the music turns slightly more urgent, as does Davies' vocal:

He needs time
He needs time for livin'
He needs time
For someone just to see him
He ain't had no lovin', For no reason or rhyme
And the whole world's above him

In a slightly bizarre lyrical twist, at this point, Davies offers his own musings on the reasons behind Rudy's crippling social inadequacies and comes up with what, in fairness, is not his most perceptive piece of psychoanalysis:

Well, it's not as though he's fat
No, there's more to it than that

I'm certain that *Weightwatchers* groups throughout the length and breadth of the land will be thanking Mr Davies for that beard-stroking piece of insight. Mind you, even in 1974, it was a terrible rhyme, we must be honest!

The music kicks up its metaphorical heels at this point, with a quick 'swoosh' straight from a Hawkwind space-rock piece leading into a short guitar solo from Hodgson, which is both superbly constructed and also significantly more overtly 'prog rock' than much of his lead guitar work. It very soon drops down again as the song continues its musical switchback ride, with Davies wearily lamenting Rudy's predicament over a restrained piano and some sultry, smoky sax accompaniment:

Rudy thought that all good things
Come to those that wait
But recently, he could see
That it may come too late

The echoing repetitions of 'too late' herald in another brief change in mood, as a forceful yet slow-paced riff is augmented by much musical ornamentation and a subtle string arrangement. This quickly dies down again to a lone piano, which almost disappears to nothing just as a mournful saxophone takes up the reins, over which can be heard the sound of railway station platform announcements. These were recorded at London's Paddington Station, where producer Ken Scott took the band on a sort of 'field trip' (there are also crowd noises on the track, which were similarly captured on a visit to Leicester Square). As these fade away, some more insistent music fades in, giving the feel of the forward momentum of a train and heralding one of the key sections of the track. Piano is joined by a funky wah-wah guitar riff sounding as close to the 'Theme From Shaft' as you could wish to get while the band hasten to join in. The bass and drums lock with the guitar to create the funk-ridden forward momentum, while the strings again come into play over the top, giving an almost discordant and other-worldly feel to proceedings. It's another masterfully constructed passage, with every instrument adding its own touches, like brushstrokes to an oil painting. This then leads into the rockiest section of the piece, Hodgson and Davies trading vocal lines in a call-and-response fashion, as Hodgson addresses Davies' defensive and agitated Rudy:

All through your life, all through the years
Nobody loved, nobody cared
So dim the light, dark are your fears
Try as I might, I can't hold back the tears
How can you live without love, it's not fair?
Someone said give, but I just didn't dare
What good advice are you waiting to hear?
Hearing's alright for them that's all there

This really gets to the crux of the matter, as we see that Rudy has simultaneously given up while also partially accepting responsibility for his own fate. He admits to his darkness and fears while also lamenting that nobody loved or cared, but then seems to allow a chink of self-realisation through. In response to the question of how he can live without love, his response is, 'Someone said give, but I just didn't dare', which sums up the tragedy of his self-defeating reticence to engage with the world brilliantly, as clearly, the world has decided not to engage with him either, leaving him frustrated and scared, but also ultimately riddled with regret. The final two lines of this verse savagely lay bare how completely he has given up on himself, as, asked about what advice he wishes to hear, he bluntly responds that 'Hearing's all right for them that's all there'. No longer is he claiming to be 'as sane as anyone', but by now, he has regressed to not only accepting his mental illness but also using it as a shield to hide behind. Musically and lyrically, this is a devastatingly effective verse and, in a sense, could be looked at as the fulcrum on which the whole album's conceptual thrust rests.

We're not done yet, however, as we head straight into another, slightly slower-paced verse as a powerful riff sees Davies outlining all of the things which Rudy must do if he is to finally help himself:

You'd better gain control now
You'd better show 'em all now
You'd better make or break now
You'd better give and take now
You'll have to push and shove now
You'll have to find some love now
You'd better gain control now

However, as soon as he finishes this intense yet well-meaning diatribe, we drop right down again, via a brief spiralling crescendo, to the sparse sound of the railway station, with what sounds like the strains of a couple of buskers playing the violin. The final denouement of the track, and essentially the whole story arc of Rudy's descent into mental disturbance and insanity, comes with Davies delivering the final verse to the accompaniment of only lonesome-sounding strings, as we hear that:

Now he's just come out the movie
Numb of all the pain
Sad, but in a while he'll soon be
Back on his train

The string accompaniment to this desolate-sounding final payoff sounds exactly like the lush soundtrack to an old black-and-white movie and, following the echoed cry of despair, which is the final line, finishes with some spiralling flourishes which evoke the final scene of such a film. It's an extraordinary way to close a track, which is one of the most complex and multi-faceted in the whole Supertramp catalogue.

And what of Rudy? Well, different theories exist as to the meaning of 'coming out the movie, numb of all the pain', with some saying it is an actual film giving him some brief escapism, but I tend to side with those who maintain that 'the movie' is a metaphor for any temporary help he might get, be it therapy, psychotic or sedative drugs or even a spell in an asylum, or secure ward, again. Whatever it may allude to, the final message is tragically clear: nothing will help permanently, and sooner or later, his issues will return again and again, and he will always end up 'back on his train'.

'If Everyone Was Listening' (4:05)

The concept at this point – if indeed it was such – seems to shift, with the final two songs not appearing to have any direct connection to the whole Rudy saga. They do, however, hang together very well as a separate 'mini concept', a suggestion which was given the thumbs up by Roger Hodgson when I raised the theory, along with my own interpretation of the songs' meanings, in 2012:

> Well, I think you nailed it! Yes, I wouldn't disagree with any of what you say there; that's pretty much how it was intended. So, in a sense, the album is two concepts in one, but probably the way I would express it is that it starts off on a personal level before ending up in a more universal, global sense.

The first of these two songs, 'If Everyone Was Listening', is Roger's fourth and final song on the album (though he did have writing input into the essentially Davies-composed title track, as we will see). The scenario of 'If Everyone Was Listening' positions the 'world stage' as, literally, a stage, with what would seem to be the world leaders of the time (but still sadly and undeniably relevant today) acting out the fate of the world in a bumbling and clueless fashion:

> The actors and jesters are here
> The stage is in darkness and clear
> For raising the curtain
> And no-one's quite certain whose play it is

This opening verse is introduced by some solitary minor-key piano, with just the slightest touch of light percussive textures added as the vocals come in. Backing vocals and a little more subtle percussion are added as the yearning chorus clearly looks back at the failure of the 'hippie dream' of peace and love, which promised so much but turned sour so quickly:

How long ago, how long?
If only we had listened then
If we'd known just how right we were going to be
For we dreamed a lot
And we schemed a lot
And we tried to sing of love before the stage fell apart

It is clear from this just what the stage metaphor represents, and as the full band come in for the chorus (still led by the piano, with Helliwell's woozy clarinet providing a strangely effective counterpoint), Hodgson laments the failure of those whose actions have the most consequences to listen to those others who have their hearts and consciences in the right place, and thus risk courting the ultimate disaster:

If everyone was listening, you know
There'd be a chance that we could save the show
Who'll be the last clown, to bring the house down?
Oh no, please no, don't let the curtain fall

Though he may plead not to let the curtain fall, there is little doubt here that the inference is that this is precisely what is going to happen. This is no song of hope offering the prospect of a green redemption just over the horizon, but a savage indictment of world politics and those in power, wrapped up in the paradoxically pleasing tones of a beautifully played melody.

A short instrumental interlude, with the piano again accompanied by some light, jazzy work from Helliwell, leads us to the next verse, as the metaphor gets further stretched, and the protagonists of disaster given a mixture of, first of all, partial understanding – but quickly followed by bitter and acid-tongued scorn:

Well, what is your costume today?
And who are the props in your play?
You're acting a part which you thought from the start
Was an honest one
Well how do you plead? An actor indeed!
Go re-learn your lines

You don't know what you've done
The finale's begun

The arrangement of these final few lines is quite brilliant, eking every single nuance of expression and meaning from every line. The words 'how do you plead? An actor indeed!' could hardly be more witheringly delivered, as all trace of the actions being honest and well-intentioned slips away in a wave of abusive bile, while the despairing 'go relearn your lines' is delivered in harmony and bathed in echo as it fades away. The damning statement that 'the finale's begun' is accompanied by the drums entering in a crescendo of dramatic portent. The chorus is repeated, with the strings added this time to give things just that extra bit of tragic pathos, as it is obvious to all by now that everyone is not, and never will be, listening.

The finale has indeed begun, and what will be this final act which 'brings the house down'? Well. The 'Crime Of The Century', naturally...

'Crime Of The Century' (5:34)

It seems clear at this point that the climactic title track of the album is essentially a direct follow-on to the scenario painted in the previous song. Another Davies composition, in essence, it is another song to benefit from some judicious collaboration, with Hodgson acknowledged to have contributed to the final piece to great effect. Indeed, it has been admitted that the song was given a little reworking and fine-tuning of sorts to fit in with this two-part 'side-concept', as we might call it. As Roger told me in 2014:

Well, 'Crime Of The Century' is certainly Rick's song, but until we had nearly finished the album, he still didn't have any words and time was running out. By then, we knew the running order and I think he took the cue directly from 'If Everyone Was Listening', and quite brilliantly, I thought. It's a fantastic lyric and quite 'un-Rick-like' in many ways. There was a little bit of collaboration in there; I had some input, though I can't really remember exactly how much. However, my forte was really in arranging the songs – everyone chipped in on that side, of course, but I had the main hand in which way the songs should be arranged, bass parts, vocal arrangements and things like that. So, that gave many of the more complex songs an element of collaboration in itself.

This largely instrumental track (with 13 lines only, the track features the briefest lyrical content on the album) is also the only one on which the vocals enter immediately, at the same time as the music begins – almost as if it the narrative is carrying straight on from where the previous song left off. Over another piano backing (again, not electric this time), Rick Davies sets the scene:

Now they're planning the crime of the century
Well what will it be?
Read all about their schemes and adventuring
Yes it's well worth the fee

Things immediately take a turn for the dramatic, however, as the band come in hard and heavy, with deep and grim-sounding backing vocals and drums which sound like the hammers of doom, as Rick's voice also becomes more guttural and intense in the darker turn in the following three lines:

So roll up and see
And they rape the universe
How they've gone from bad to worse

This straight away seems to tie in with the destructive individuals 'bringing the house down' in 'If Everyone Was Listening', and to reinforce that connection, there is a direct allusion to the same stage/theatre metaphor in the 'Roll up and see' line. Quite contrary to the hope that everyone could, at some point, be listening to the words of those urging sanity, things have, in fact, 'gone from bad to worse', and the inference is clear that the final disaster and the fall of the curtain is imminent. The 'last clown' will soon be bringing the house down.

But there's a twist still to come in this effectively concise lyric, as the music returns to the piano backing from the initial verse, fleshed out now with drums and some sparse instrumentation. Who is the figurative 'last clown' who we can all blame for this unspoken global catastrophe which is to befall us all?

Who are these men of lust, greed, and glory?
Rip off the masks and let's see
But that's not right – oh no, what's the story?
There's you and there's me
(That can't be right!)

The masks of the players are removed, only for our own faces to be revealed beneath. In the final analysis, when the finger-pointing is done and over, the unpalatable truth implied here is that, to some extent, we are all culpable as a species for the fate of mankind. None of us can claim that our hands are completely clean of blood. Is this an ecological disaster? Can any of us say with honesty that we have never done anything to harm the environment? Is it a nuclear catastrophe? Who among us can say that we have not shrugged our shoulders and hoped that it will all turn out for the best? It's a fascinating moral and ethical debate which is offered up, and to do so in the space of only a dozen lines is brilliant songwriting. Note also the final, barely audible, payoff with the denial in the remark 'that can't be right' – which, once again, harks back to 'you're bloody well right', and the subsequent ignoring of that valid complaint by those in authority (plus, if one wishes, this connection can be extended to 'not quite right!' in 'Asylum'). This could be coincidental, but on the other hand, the meticulously crafted nature of Supertramp's compositions tends not to thrive on such things, and it may well be that a link is being drawn somehow between the impotent raging of the complainant about the ills of society and the subsequent final reckoning, which drags us all into its grasp. After all, as Roger did state, as detailed above, 'the way I would express it is that it starts off on a personal level before ending up in a more universal, global sense'.

That may be the end of the lyrical content, but musically speaking, we are barely getting started, with only 80 seconds of the track elapsed. Immediately, the vocal ends, Roger comes in with a 45-second guitar solo, first a single guitar and then double-tracked, which is a perfect bridge into the final section of the track, as a simple but brilliantly effective staccato piano figure comes in, soon joined by sparse, yet once again, beautifully nuanced bass and drum accompaniment. The tension is being ratcheted up, as the listener is aware that at any moment, the dam will burst, as it finally does after another 45 seconds or so of this building tension. The whole band come in, with the strings again bringing the grand icing on the cake, increasing in intensity until John Helliwell's masterful saxophone solo takes over to bring the song into its final coda. At around the five-minute mark, a lengthy and gradual fade-out begins (so lengthy that the album cover underestimates the time by around 14 seconds). This is the only way that this album could possibly end, slowly dying away into the ether, leaving us still waiting for that curtain to finally fall – or will it be rescued at the last moment? The secret is in what we can no longer hear after the music has finally ebbed away.

That's the way to close an album as masterfully constructed as this one, and the world didn't take too long to agree on the fact.

The Impact Of The Crime – Release, Reception And Touring

The music was all done and in the can, so to speak, but there remained the question of how to package this release in the days when vinyl ruled the musical roost and album covers were intrinsically linked to the music found within. Indeed, as evidenced by the work of the likes of Roger Dean and the Hipgnosis design team, the right image, especially if associated with a particular band or genre, such as Roger Dean's close association with Yes, could and did significantly impact sales. At a time when the only chance of hearing an album before buying it rested on singles being released, unlikely airplay of album tracks on a rather safe and staid radio environment or the occasional record shops which offered listening booths, people would very often make a purchase based almost entirely on the cover design and the music it evoked (I know, having done this myself many times in those days – often happily but occasionally disastrously!).

The photographer responsible for the cover image was Paul Wakefield, who would go on to do Supertramp's follow-up album *Crisis? What Crisis?* as well as several other highly regarded album covers, including *Heaven And Hell* by Vangelis, *Dinner At The Ritz* by City Boy and *The Scream* by Siouxsie And The Banshees. *Crime Of The Century*, however, was his first album cover assignment. He was engaged by the art director Fabio Nicoli and basically given free rein to his imagination. Invited into the studio, he was given the lyrics to read and asked to think of what might make an appropriate cover image. Interviewed for *The Album Cover Hall Of Fame* website in 2014, he recalled:

It was a combination of the line, 'when they haunt me and taunt me in my cage', from the song 'Asylum' and asking myself what an appropriate sentence could be for 'the crime of the century'. I came up with quite a few ideas – one being a stabbed teddy bear in an alleyway, with all its guts spilling out (those were the days!). Needless to say, they didn't go for that one. Another was a prison cell window floating in space with a person silently screaming through the bars. They liked that, and after a bit more deliberation, we decided on the idea of both hands on the bars, as it shows a resignation to fate that the other didn't have. It felt like there would be no reprieve.

For the setup of the shot, he got a friend of his to make a set of polished aluminium bars and attach them to a stand, and then, he had his brother pose with his hands holding the bars. To achieve the right effect, his hands were whitened by makeup, as retouching with the likes of Photoshop was, of course, decades away! This made the whole process far more complex than young modern-day photographers would imagine, as he explained:

I chose to do it as a double exposure in-camera, as I'd been working with that method for a couple of years already. Once it was all set up, I drew the bars and hands on the ground-glass screen – my brother having to keep very still while I then shot 12 sheets of transparency film on an old mahogany 5x7 camera that once belonged to an Indian Maharaja. The film was taped into the hinged wooden dark slides to stop them from moving during the whole process.

Things were still far from done, as there was the matter of the space background. Of course, today, the bars would simply be dropped into an image of a starry background, but in 1974, things had to be more imaginative, and the effect was produced by taking a black card background and actually making a lot of holes in it! Wakefield again:

I then made a starscape by pricking various-sized holes in a 30x40-inch piece of black card. I placed the camera in front of this, lit from behind, and then had to cover up all the holes that were inside the drawn area of bars/hands to avoid double-exposing over the image already recorded on film. During the whole shoot, the studio was blacked out. I then processed the double-exposed sheets of film, and I think there were six sheets that were pretty well perfect.

The result was beyond successful, with the finished design going on to become one of the most iconic album cover images ever produced and entirely inseparable in the imagination from the music on the album. The album cover was originally intended to be a gatefold, but very disappointingly, this was abandoned, as the unfolded cover makes a beautiful, complete image, with the stars spreading from the front to the back. At the bottom of the rear cover, below the album credits, there can be seen a bizarre image of the band standing naked, looking up at the stars and holding top hats and suits as if from a wedding to hide their own 'exposure'!

According to Wakefield, that shot was originally intended for when there was an inner gatefold planned, and another part of that initial plan is carried over to the lyric sheet insert, which has a photo on the reverse of the jackets and top hats in front of the stars again, presumably abandoned by their oddly naked owners. When I spoke to Roger Hodgson in 2014, he emphasised his admiration for the design but couldn't resist an aside referencing this surreal bit of photography along the way:

> The design was just perfect from the word go. I mean, the hands on the bars can represent so many of the songs; it can represent 'Hide In Your Shell', with the yearning to escape; it can represent 'Dreamer', with being trapped in your head; and, of course, the prison bars equating to the Crime itself. The space backdrop suggests the theme of feeling lost, alienated and not feeling at home or belonging. There are so many ways it fits the spirit of the record. And the shot with the top hats and tails... (laughs)... yeah, a lot of great themes on there!

The lyric sheet in itself had an interesting design, as the lines sung by Hodgson and Davies, respectively, were printed in white and yellow according to who sang them – not just the main lead vocal, but every line which one of them traded within another's song. This is the reason why the credits on the back cover have the word 'Vocals' against Davies printed in yellow – the sole yellow word in an otherwise entirely white set of notes. It is immediately obvious on seeing the insert, but I'm sure I cannot have been the only one confused when I first saw the record in the racks when it was released, assuming that it perhaps meant that Davies was the main vocalist and that the yellow print was emphasising that. Now, of course, it is another peculiarity which is intrinsically linked with the cover.

When the album was released, its success took even the band by surprise, reaching number four in the UK album charts after the first two albums had made no placing whatsoever. It also reached number four in Canada, five in Germany, the top 20 in Australia and New Zealand and even managed number 38 in the American *Billboard* chart, beating their previous best of 158 for the debut album by some considerable distance. They would go on to have higher chart placings, but following the complete failure of the previous two albums, it represented a rebirth which was little short of miraculous and spoke volumes for the quality of the record since there was almost no existing audience to build upon. It was the very definition of an album being the launchpad for an artist's career, and they never really looked back. 'Dreamer' managed number 13 on the UK singles charts, while the flip side 'Bloody Well Right' hit 35 in the US, narrowly outdoing the album position.

The touring for the album was a big difference for the band. Previously, their audience had been a fairly minuscule one, and their gigs reflected this, but with the release of *Crime Of The Century*, and its success, they ambitiously went straight for headline shows in theatre venues. Supporting another act was ruled out because of the scale of the show, utilising back projections and the like, so they went in as big as they could, even if it meant losing money in the process. In an appearance on *In The Studio With Redbeard*, Roger Hodgson remembered what he considered as perhaps the highlight of the show – the film accompanying 'Rudy':

It was a train ride that was filmed; there was a camera put on a train back in the 1950s, I guess, and it was shot at high speed to make the train look like it was going about 500 miles per hour. It was the train ride from London to Brighton, and we managed to procure it from the BBC. It lasted for about three minutes … on the front of a train, hurtling down these railway lines at about 500 mph. Now, if you can imagine that blown up so that it filled the whole back of the stage, you were on that train. It was amazing, and the music going 'chaka-chaka-chaka' with it – it was a very important part of the show.

In the same interview, Roger spoke about the decision to headline the shows, stating that there was no other choice unless they wanted to 'ditch about three-quarters of the show'. They had, he says, enormous support from A&M records, agents and prompters, who just 'took a shot', but things were sometimes less successful in America, where he remembers times when they would turn up in a city for a show, find out 'only about 200 tickets had been sold' and they would go out on the street handing out tickets just to get a crowd in and make it a good show. It paid off, and the reactions to the show gave their reputation another fresh boost after the album.

The first show the band played showcasing the album was a one-off performance at the Kings Road Theatre, London, on 22 September 1974, a media showcase a month before the release of the record. The actual tour proper began on 18 October (one week before release) at Swansea University. This was the first of an astonishing 36 dates in the UK, lasting until 11 February 1975 in Torquay (how many bands stop off there on their tour itineraries these days?). Following three European dates in Denmark, France and Holland, one more UK show was performed, with an appearance at Hammersmith Odeon on 9 March – this was recorded and released 40 years later as part of the 40th Anniversary CD Edition of *Crime Of The Century*. Following that, it was across the Atlantic for a further 26 shows in the US and Canada, running from 4 April in Milwaukee through to 17 August in Montreal – meaning that the band spent four and a half months touring across North America. In actual fact, there were a couple of significant breaks – between 26 April and 25 May and later between 20 June and 31 July, there are no shows recorded as taking place, this reportedly being largely because Roger Hodgson injured his hand while the band were on the Californian leg, and several dates had to be cancelled. This enabled them to do a little work for the next album, *Crisis? What Crisis?*, though to all intents and purposes, it was recorded quickly as soon as the US tour ended. The final shows billed as part of the *Crime* tour were a couple of festival appearances – the Reading Festival on 23 August and an event billed as The Big Rock Show 1975 in Munich on 4 September. There were precisely two months off the road before the tour promoting the *Crisis? What Crisis?* album began on 4 November.

The shows, of course, included the whole of the *Crime Of The Century* album played in sequence, but in between the performances of 'Asylum' and 'Dreamer' – at the halfway point of the album – four songs from the as yet unrecorded *Crisis? What Crisis?* album were performed (as documented on the Hammersmith recording). These songs were 'Sister Moonshine', 'Another Man's Woman', 'Just A Normal Day' and 'Lady', though there was also a bizarre rendition of the old Perry Como standard 'A – You're Adorable', AKA 'The Alphabet Song', which no-one would have expected! Reliable setlists from earlier on the tour are sketchy and hard to find, but there are several references to these songs being performed at a significant number of different shows.

At around this time, there was one occasion which really emphasised just how much the band had entered the UK national consciousness when they were actually referenced in an episode of the soap opera institution which is, and was, *Coronation Street*. The characters Gail and Tricia were making plans for a party when it was mentioned that one of the male guests was 'going to bring his Supertramp' – as if that was a big thing which would draw people to a party in mid-'70s England. The closest parallel would be that this was somewhat akin to appearing on *The Simpsons* today. Clearly, Supertramp had arrived.

The Fallout – The Highs And Lows Of Following Up The Album

As is always the case with a 'breakout' album of such success, it takes the band concerned to a whole new level of expectation – and record company pressure was high for a rapid follow-up album. Uriah Heep had this issue, for example, when *Demons And Wizards* was followed up in absurd haste within months by *The Magician's Birthday*, which suffered a little from being rushed. There are always odd exceptions – Pink Floyd were somehow allowed two years to follow up *Dark Side Of The Moon* with *Wish You Were Here* by a patient and benevolent EMI, and the quality showed as a result. Supertramp were practically chased into the studio the moment they finished the *Crime* tour, with nowhere near enough new material having been written, and as a result, they had to delve into the stockpile of songs already written, at least by the astoundingly prolific Hodgson. With Davies, it was a different matter, as he rarely wrote more songs than were required at the current time. In 2014, Roger had an interesting take on the rushed nature of the recording and the eventual result:

> It wasn't so much the record company wanting to cash in, which rushed it, more the fact that we had a tour booked and we had to move the release date forward to accommodate that. We certainly felt the difference, though, after the luxury we had on *Crime Of The Century*, having the two months in the farmhouse to write, rehearse, demo at our leisure and go into the recording process totally prepared. It was a very different situation with *Crisis*, I can tell you that! Interestingly, however, although for years *Crisis, What Crisis?* was my biggest frustration, owing to the way the songs were arranged and produced so quickly that they couldn't fulfil their potential; nowadays, it's actually my favourite Supertramp album, my favourite collection of songs.

Regardless of the way the album has grown in Roger's affections over the years, it was certainly the case that, when the album was released in November 1975, it sagged somewhat under the weight of public expectation, leading to a fair amount of negative comparisons to its predecessor. This is an entirely expected response after a particular triumph, of course – Led Zeppelin hit the same critical reception with *Led Zeppelin III* and *Houses Of The Holy*, following their landmark second and fourth albums, to name one example, though both have been retrospectively valued far higher in the decades since. The truth with *Crisis? What Crisis?* is probably somewhere in the middle, to be fair. There is no way that I would rank it in the same league as *Crime Of The Century*, but it does contain some of the band's more enduring songs, even if, in some cases, they would prove to be better in the live environment.

Among the tracks which would go on to become well-regarded by fans are Davies' 'Ain't Nobody But Me' (a song which was actually written 'to order' during an enforced break in the recording when it became necessary to get some more material quickly) and 'Another Man's Woman', and Hodgson's album-closing pair, the philosophical musings of 'The Meaning' and the fragile tenderness of 'Two Of Us'. Perhaps the most enduring song from the album, however, would end up being another Hodgson-penned one, the lyrically intriguing 'A Soapbox Opera', with its characters of Father Washington and Sister Robinson. I asked Roger about the inspiration for these characters and whether or not they were based on actual people:

Those characters weren't based on any specific real people, no. That song was sort of my take on traditional religion, done in a slightly tongue-in-cheek way because I personally hadn't found any real answers from what I was taught growing up at school and church. Nothing they said really touched me, so Father Washington and Sister Robinson sort of illustrate that. I love some of the imagery in that song, like the 'collecting sinners in an old tin cup' bit – I remember in church as a child, passing the cup around as we all put our pennies into it. The characters were just people from my imagination, which I used to try to bring the concept to life a little.

If the music on the album was not always entirely memorable, the same could not be said for the album cover design, which managed to be just as iconic and memorable as that of *Crime Of The Century*, and for good reason – the work was by none other than Paul Wakefield again. The original concept for the cover actually came from Rick Davies, as well as the title itself, which comes from a phrase used in the 1973 film *The Day Of The Jackal*. As John Helliwell described it, 'It was Rick that came up with the name *Crisis? What Crisis?*, and one day, when we were sitting around Scorpio Studio, he came in with this sketch of a guy in a deck chair under an umbrella with all this chaos going on around him'. Wakefield was sent out to gather the visual material for the cover, and he returned with grim landscapes of the Welsh Valleys – back when the pits were open and the skyline was less than idyllic, to say the least. He then photographed a model in a studio shot sitting under a bright yellow umbrella in a deckchair, sipping a drink and caring not one iota for the grey, oppressive vistas spread out around him. The juxtaposition of the brightly colourful deckchair character against the monochromatic gloom of the wider world is a brilliant visual image and went on to be recognised as such.

By this time, with the sheer amount of touring the band had done on the back of *Crime Of The Century* in much bigger venues than their pre-*Crime* days, they were becoming more confident on stage. Quoted in *Sounds* in late 1975, however, Rick Davies did temper this with a slight note of caution:

I think it's taken almost this long to get completely on top of it without worrying about little knobs and switches, so in a way, you can go out there and relax. There are only a couple of numbers that worry me technically. Once you start getting on top of it, you have to be careful that you're not going to become complacent. When you stop thinking, 'Is it going to be alright?', and start thinking, 'This is going to be a piece of piss' – it's only on the last gigs that I've thought, 'this is nothing, I can do this easy', but you soon get brought down to earth about it all.

The shows on the *Crisis* tour included several tracks from that album, as one might expect, but tellingly, still leaned heavily on the *Crime Of The Century* material. While accurate setlists are hard to come by, with some contradictions and incomplete listings abounding, several reports indicate the whole of the *Crime* album being performed, with perhaps only five or six from *Crisis*.

Speaking to *Sounds* in 1976, John Helliwell referenced the fact that the band's audiences tended very much towards respectfully listening rather than the more enthusiastically 'rowdy' behaviour experienced by other bands and that they actually enjoyed having people listen attentively to what they were doing. He remembered one favourite incident:

But the best one was somewhere in England, and we asked if everyone was listening – and we stopped, and there was about a five-second period of quietness from the audience and then someone yelled out, 'Per-fect!!' Everybody clapped.

By the time the tour ended in June 1976, following an Australia/New Zealand leg, there was clearly a concerted decision to take a long enough break from the road to allow the next album to be properly planned and worked on without schedules hanging over the work like the lowering of a spiked ceiling. To that end, there were no shows planned until February 1977, while work commenced on the next album *Even In The Quietest Moments*. Indeed, at the end of the tour, the band took four much-needed months off to rest and prepare before recording commenced in November 1976. Most of the work took place in Caribou Studios in Colorado, though with that particular facility only being available for two months, the work had to be completed in Los Angeles in January. The most significant change this time out was the decision by the band to produce the album themselves, dispensing entirely with the services of Ken Scott, whose work as producer had been so pivotal to *Crime Of The Century* – if less so for *Crisis? What Crisis?*, owing to the rushed nature of its creation. The resulting album came out to mixed reviews in the press, but it remains popular among fans, with many of the more 'prog rock'-oriented fanbase rating it and *Crime* as the band's two best studio albums.

By this time, Hodgson and Davies were writing entirely separately, without even the modest crossover and collaboration evident on 'School' and 'Crime Of The Century', and Davies would be quoted as saying, somewhat tellingly as regards the relationship between the pair – which would later break down entirely:

It takes a lot more energy to argue a point because of the strength of the individual now. If I look at a song of Roger's and I think it's wrong, I've got to be really one hundred per cent there to fight that. Usually, I just don't have the energy to do so because I see it blowing up into a huge misunderstanding.

An interesting feature of the album's running order is that, in the same way as *Crime Of The Century*, the two writers' songs are alternated, with Hodgson contributing tracks one, three, five and seven and Davies two, four and six – once again, odd numbers for Roger and even for Rick. One thing the album managed, which *Crisis* had failed to do, was to give the band another hit. The opening track, Roger's 'Give A Little Bit', reached the top 30 in the UK and US and the top ten in several other countries – not a smash hit exactly, but it has gone on to become easily one of the band's best-known songs.

Roger's spiritual side was illustrated by the mantra-like 'Babaji', while the title track, also written by him, was a beautifully constructed piece. Davies had only three songs, but all were of good quality, with 'Loverboy' and the gently contemplative 'Downstream' showcasing very different sides to his writing, and 'From Now On' boasting a call-and-response coda which would be honed and improved on stage to make it a live highlight on future tours.

Perhaps the highlight of the album, certainly for the band's proggier-minded fans, was the closing 'Fool's Overture', Roger's 12-minute epic of historical rumination. It used samples, such as Winston Churchill's famous 1940 'We shall never surrender' speech. In 2012, I asked Roger for his thoughts on the piece, its meaning and relevance to him, and the use of that Churchill quote:

'Fool's Overture' – that's sort of a collage of history if you like. When I wrote that, in the mid-seventies, memories of the Second World War were still very strong in people's consciousness, much more so than they are today, so the Churchill sample had great resonance. The lyric in there which goes, 'history recalls how great the fall can be', is sort of about the fall of Man, and the best way to illustrate that at that time was the Second World War, so that's really where the Churchill thing and the sound effects fit in. The other part of 'Fool's Overture' is the 'Called the man a fool' section, and that's about Jesus, so there's a verse there that sort of switches between the two meanings. I don't want to pin it down too much because people might have their own meanings that they see in it, so I don't want to spoil anything like that, but that's a little of what it means to me. It still amazes me how that song came together actually, because I had two or three instrumental passages which somehow all slotted together perfectly and created this epic, you know? When I play it today, it still has this great innate power to it; it can be electrifying – and indeed, I close my current show with it.

The album, again, boasted an intriguing and eye-catching cover photo showing a grand piano on a cold mountainside covered in a layer of snow. On the piano can be seen a piece of sheet music which reads 'Fool's Overture', although interestingly, those who know about these things (and presumably have excellent eyesight) claim that the music actually written there is the American national anthem 'The Star Spangled Banner'. If true, this must certainly rank as one of the most subtle and somewhat mischievous pieces of political satire to have made its way onto a popular album cover! Another claim over the years has been that the snow must surely be false, or the photo doctored, as it would not stick in such a way to the angled open lid without sliding off, but Roger, in that same 2012 interview, entirely refuted this accusation:

> Ha, it must have been glued on! No, in all honesty, that shot was absolutely real; you know, it wasn't staged at all. They actually took a piano up into the mountains in Colorado and left it there overnight, during which time it snowed. I know what you mean about the lid, but I can only assume it froze in place. It was certainly heavy snow! But the covers were so important back then; it was an integral part of the whole album package and we took it very seriously.

In actual fact, the precise location of the piano was a place called the Eldora Mountain Resort, which was a ski area near the Caribou Studio where the band were recording at the time, and although it was a real piano, it did have most of its inner workings removed to make it at least manageable to transport up there! Back then, album cover designers had to suffer for their art, and PhotoShop only meant somewhere you went to get your holiday pictures developed...

The tour began in February 1977 in London and ran through to November, where it also finished in the capital, at St Mary's College. In between had been a string of other UK shows, a number of dates in mainland Europe and an extensive jaunt around Canada and the US. Canada was, by now, one of the territories which had taken the band to their hearts, with *Even In The Quietest Moments* hitting number one in the Canadian album charts (it made 12 in the UK and 16 in the US), and they also sent the 'Give A Little Bit' single into the top ten. Once again, the majority of *Crime Of The Century* was included in the set, with the bulk of the remainder from the new album and a few selections from *Crisis? What Crisis?*.

By most standards, the album was a success, both artistically and commercially. What it had not yet done, however, was to move the band's profile substantially upwards and take them up to another level of success. Since the immediate impact of *Crime Of The Century*, it could probably safely be said that the band had remained a popular act, if not quite in the top tier, and were respected by their fanbase rather than really capturing the public's imagination and becoming a ubiquitous radio-airwaves phenomenon. One thing Roger Hodgson has said is that he is a strong believer in the 'rule of three', in that the number seems to occur very obviously on what one might call a cosmic scale, with things tending to 'come in threes' or the saying that 'third time's the charm'. He had used, as an example, the fact that the first two Supertramp albums had been released without much success before the third, *Crime*, had shifted the playing field entirely. Since then, there had been two more successful, if not game-changing, albums following it. It was time for the rule of three to be tested again … and so it was to be in some style!

Breakfast Of Champions – The World Awakens To Supertramp

One thing which had become clear to the band was that, despite the excellence of much of the material on the last two albums, they had begun to garner a reputation as being somewhat too 'serious' and failing to possess the inclination or ability to produce more upbeat – and by extension, more mass-market commercial – material. This was at odds with their live shows, which, by now, had begun to feature the genial and good-humoured figure of John Helliwell to provide some verbal and visual lightness of touch. It is true that Rick Davies was never very likely to start cracking a few jokes at the keyboard, but defining the band by an individual member's somewhat sterner impression would be a mistake.

Not that there was necessarily a specific agenda to tweak the overall mood of the album, as Roger Hodgson explained to me in 2012:

Well, it wasn't so much a conscious decision for the direction of the album. The thing is, all of our albums came at a different time and had their own character – *Crime Of The Century*, for example, was very much a 'listening album', whereby you could put the headphones on and really get into it, whereas *Breakfast In America* was more of an album that you could put on in the car or whatever and it would put a smile on your face. When we came to getting the tracks together for the album, it was never a case of writing to order, to fit a certain mould. For my part, I was always very prolific, and I always had a backlog of songs to choose from – I still do, to be honest. Rick, on the other hand, was the opposite – he would always come in with his five or six songs, so what I would do would be to dip into the collection of songs I had ready and see which of mine matched his, which was very much the case with the *Breakfast In America* album. The actual title song 'Breakfast In America' was written years before – in fact, it could have been on *Crime Of The Century*, but it definitely wouldn't have fit there! When it came to *Breakfast In America*, though, with the songs Rick had ready, it did fit. We weren't looking for hits as such with that album, but what we were looking for was more of an upbeat, feel-good atmosphere to it, and that's how that particular collection of songs ended up on there.

In fact, when the recording was first conceived, there was reportedly talk of it being a concept album, with its central idea revolving around the two songwriters and their own conflicting ideals. This was, perhaps wisely, abandoned, and it is indeed hard to imagine the somewhat weightier tone of such an album giving rise to the raft of hit singles and radio staples which eventually arose from *Breakfast In America*. All of this still hasn't prevented people from speculating as to whether there is a concept behind the final album relating to American culture and its commercialism and global spread, but the band have always very much denied this. It does, to my mind, seem somewhat of a stretch, though it is possible to see in some of the material and the album cover where the idea arose, and even the band members have accepted that there were a few references to general Americana, though they stress these were not premeditated.

The album was begun by Davies and Hodgson each producing rough demos of their individually written material, performed by themselves alone at the piano. There was then a further round of demos recorded on eight-track tape in California in 1978. These supplied the basis for most of the final arrangements when the album was recorded, also in California, at The Village recording studio in West Los Angeles. The only track to be brought in following those initial eight-track recordings was Roger Hodgson's 'Take The Long Way Home'. The album produced four successful singles, all being top ten in either the UK or the US – three of them being Hodgson compositions. His 'The Logical Song' was the first single release and the biggest seller overall, hitting number seven in the UK and six on the US *Billboard* chart. The title track followed this, reaching nine in the UK chart, though only 62 in the US. A Davies composition, 'Goodbye Stranger', managed the opposite, hitting 15 in the US but only managing 57 in the UK, while the final single release, 'Take The Long Way Home', was not released back home in Britain, though it did reach number ten in the US. Interestingly, a live version of the song was put out as a European single the following year, including the UK.

For the majority of mainstream radio listeners, at least in the UK, the album – and to a lesser extent, the band as well – remains defined by the two big hits 'The Logical Song' and 'Breakfast In America', making this popular image of the band synonymous with Hodgson's voice and the similarly jaunty, upbeat electric piano base which both tracks possess. In terms of the band's own fanbase, this was broadened massively by the album's success, especially in the US, where it eclipsed their previous standing by topping the *Billboard* chart and going on to be verified quadruple platinum with 4,000,000 in America alone. It also made number three in the UK, with domestic sales of 300,000, and topped the album charts in ten countries. Roger Hodgson's 'rule of three' had paid out in spades once again, as the third album following the *Crime Of The Century* breakthrough.

However, there was more to the album than the admittedly heavily weighted, lighter, up-tempo material, with Hodgson's deeper, more spiritually reflective songs 'Lord Is It Mine' and the closing epic 'Child Of Vision' of particular appeal to fans of the band's more serious, 'progressive' side. Roger agreed that these songs were highlights for him when he spoke with me in 2012: 'Yes, well, that certainly fits in with my view, actually. When I write a song, I never look for the 'hit'; I just look for a strong song. 'Lord Is It Mine' is probably my favourite track from the album and I love playing 'Child Of Vision' live – it's a very powerful song'.

The album cover, designed by Mike Doud and Mick Haggerty, is a rather clever image. Displayed as if photographed from an aeroplane window, it shows what initially appears to be merely a photo of a buxom yellow-clad waitress holding a glass of orange juice aloft. However, a closer examination reveals her to be a representation of the Statue Of Liberty, with the menu clasped to her chest and the orange juice the torch, while the scene behind her is the Manhattan aerial view represented entirely with breakfast cutlery and crockery and assorted boxes and other accoutrements. The waitress, complete with the nametag 'Libby', was actually an American actress named Kate Murtagh, who eventually passed away in 2017 aged 96. She is also seen on the back cover serving breakfast to the band members in a rather chaotic style.

It's an extremely smart design for sure, though it did give rise to rather a far-fetched conspiracy theory decades later when it was claimed that it 'predicted' the 9/11 attack on the Twin Towers of the World Trade Centre. The towers are depicted clearly by what appear to be two piles of boxes of some sort, but it was claimed to be significant that the orange juice ('the colour of fire', if you have some very bright orangey fire) is directly in front of them, and the letters U and P arising from them resemble, in a mirror, the numbers nine and 11. Should you require more convincing of this extremely shaky premise, the title of the album is said to reference the 8:45 'breakfast time' of the first attack. Oh, and there is also a plane on the inner sleeve, heading from the letter T toward the city. Of course, it is actually heading straight for the Statue Of Liberty, but let's not let details get in the way. Even if anyone were to buy into this, 22 years seems quite the wait between plan, hint and eventual payoff…

The tour to promote the album was unsurprisingly an extensive one, with 119 shows between March and December 1979. Indeed, Roger Hodgson's daughter Heidi was actually born in a mobile home trailer in the parking lot of the San Diego Sports Arena prior to a show in April, just 12 minutes before the scheduled show time, with Roger assisting with the birth – not the most 'rock 'n' roll' preparation for a gig perhaps, but in its own way, typically 'Supertramp'. They were apparently 34 minutes late starting the show, but given the circumstances, this was hardly a delay of Axl Rose proportions...

The shift in the band's popularity can be easily seen by the fact that the US had 56 of those gigs and Canada 16, while the UK only got four – held over four nights at Wembley Arena, without any shows elsewhere in the country. Shows at the Pavilion De Paris were recorded and used for a live album titled *Paris*. Most of the tracks came from a show on 29 November 1979, and the album came out almost exactly a year later on 30 November 1980. If ever there was evidence for the continued popularity of and high regard for the *Crime Of The Century* album, it can be seen in the tracklist of this double vinyl release, which contained seven out of the eight tracks on the *Crime* album, along with a total of eight from the other three put together, including only three from *Breakfast In America*, surprisingly. There was also an outing for the B-side to the 'Lady' single, 'You Started Laughing', making up the 16 tracks. The only *Crime* song not to make the cut is 'If Everyone Was Listening', while 'School' and 'Crime Of The Century' open and close the show as they did the original album.

Several tracks performed at the recorded shows missed the cut for the double vinyl release; these were 'Give A Little Bit', 'Another Man's Woman', 'Downstream', 'Even In The Quietest Moments', 'Goodbye Stranger' and – perhaps most disappointingly – 'Child Of Vision'. 'Give A Little Bit' was planned for inclusion, but when listening to the recordings, the band were unimpressed by the quality of the performances and simply couldn't agree on one they considered good enough. It is interesting to note that when deciding which of the other five songs to exclude for space reasons, none of the *Crime Of The Century* selections were cut, while every other album loses at least one. All of these missing tracks (including 'Give A Little Bit', which was perhaps harshly judged) eventually surfaced on the 2015 2CD/DVD audio-visual set *Live In Paris '79*.

Following the tour promoting the album's release, appetite was obviously keen for a follow-up record, with the clear potential to build upon the enormous success of *Breakfast In America*. In actual fact, this next release, *...Famous Last Words...*, would not appear until October 1982 – a full three and a half years after the release of *Breakfast* and two years even after the space-filling *Paris*, by which time, much of the momentum had understandably stalled. At this point, the band were – unbeknownst to the public – struggling to retain a united front against the rapidly deteriorating relations between the twin leaders Hodgson and Davies, who, by then, were reportedly barely on speaking terms.

Directly following the *Breakfast* tour, everyone concerned agreed that a break was needed, so a short hiatus was planned. For Roger Hodgson, this was a very significant time, as he took the opportunity to relocate with his wife and daughter to California, where they also had a son before the band regrouped again. It is generally agreed now that, quite naturally, the geographic remoteness of Roger on the West Coast of America and the rest of the band still on the other side of the Atlantic most probably contributed to a sense of divisiveness – a sense which reached its inevitable conclusion when Roger Hodgson eventually left the band in 1982. As Roger told me in 2012:

The spirit within the band up to *Breakfast In America* was fantastic, but after the *Breakfast* tour, the fun seemed to go out of it, and by the time of *...Famous Last Words...,* I just needed to get away and take a break; I was disillusioned with the band and the whole music industry to tell you the truth. When I left the band, I also left Los Angeles, which is where the music business was centred, and I relocated to Northern California with my family to take some time for myself and for us to be together and just do something else for a while. I built a studio so that I could still release albums occasionally, and I just used the time to raise my kids and get back to real life, if you like.

Prior to the split, however, there were some hopes that the *...Famous Last Words...* album could bring back some sense of unity and, indeed, inspiration to the band, but the resulting record was patchy, to say the least, with even the band accepting this in hindsight. Commencing in November 1981, the album sessions were slow and tortuous, taking until mid-1982 to complete. Much of the recording was done at Hodgson's own home studio, Unicorn, with some additional work and overdubs taking place in three different Los Angeles studios. Rick Davies, in particular, recorded a significant amount of his own parts away from Unicorn. By this time, Roger and his wife had a newborn son, Andrew, and it is understandable that he would have wanted to stay at home as much as possible, but it is a keen illustration of how the priorities of various band members had changed within a decade or less.

The generally received wisdom is that the album ended up being a rather compromised affair, matching up to neither Davies nor Hodgson's original vision for it. One extremely notable omission was the then-ten-minute 'Brother Where You Bound', which would go on to be used as the title track to the band's first post-Hodgson record, by which time, it had expanded to 16 minutes. Roger expanded on this to me in 2012:

> Well, things had got difficult at the time, certainly – not necessarily between Rick and me as such, but between all of us, really. The band had gone past its peak artistically, and everyone was beginning to think individually rather than collectively, which had a very detrimental effect on the band's spirit. ...*Famous Last Words...* was a last-ditch attempt to see if we could still make something magic happen, but it was a miserable album to make for all concerned, I think. The atmosphere was bad in the studio, and the album ended up as a great disappointment as a result – it was such a compromise in the end, it really could have been a great album. We had some great songs there, but when it became clear how difficult it was becoming, we just ended up using the songs which we felt we could finish, which were generally the simpler songs.

When the album finally appeared in October 1982, it was immediately clear that 'generally the simpler songs' was an accurate assessment, and reviews were generally not favourable. To be fair, the album does have its moments – Roger Hodgson's 'It's Raining Again' has gone on to become one of the band's most well-known songs, and the closing pairing of Davies's 'Waiting So Long' and Hodgson's 'Don't Leave Me Now' provide an excellent finish to the record (they are, coincidentally, the only songs to come in at over six minutes). Elsewhere, though, there is undeniable filler material, and it sounds like a band that are playing it safe and under no illusions that they are not producing their finest work.

The album's title is a deliberate nod to the fact that it was likely to be the 'last hurrah' for the classic lineup at least, and the artwork ties into this. The front cover shows a tightrope walker heading away from the viewer's point of view, while in the immediate foreground, a large pair of scissors stands poised to cut the rope from under him. With art by Mike Dowd, it is a colourful and attractive-looking image at least. The rest of the packaging is less engaging, with the back cover showing five white top hats (as worn by the endangered tightrope walker) tumbling down beside the song titles and the inner sleeve having the lyrics on one side and the various band members appearing to be walking on tightropes on the other. Roger Hodgson confirmed in 2015 that he and Davies decided on the title as they knew they weren't going to do another record together, but John Helliwell, speaking in 1986 and quoted in *The Supertramp Book* (Martin Melhuish), had a slightly less equivocal take on it:

We wanted a phrase that bore some relationship with what we were doing but was enigmatic at the same time. We always like to have enigmatic titles, such as *Crime Of The Century*. We thought this last LP was going to be real quick. We thought we were going to rehearse it and record it real quick and it ended up taking longer than any other, so we had to eat our words again. For the past three or four LPs, we've been saying, 'Let's be well prepared'. So, the title sprung out of that as well. I can't remember who first thought of it. The graphic design came directly from the title.

Of course, given that he was speaking at a time when the band had recently begun their continuation as an ongoing entity without Hodgson, it is understandable that he might want to lessen the focus on any suggestion that the band might have been considering splitting up.

There was one final world tour with the 'classic' lineup, as the band embarked on 65 shows, dubbed the *Famous Last Tour*, between June and September 1983. Roger Hodgson's departure was officially announced in March 1983, after the album's release but before the tour began. Actually, it would be inaccurate to call this the final tour with the 'classic' lineup, as the band were augmented by two extra musicians – Scott Page and Fred Mandel – who, between them, covered extra keyboards, guitar, sax and vocals to fill out the sound and enable some songs to be played, which had previously proved impractical ('Gone Hollywood' being one example). It seemed to work artistically since, in stark contrast to the thumbs down the album had received from the critics, the live shows attracted overwhelmingly positive reviews.

The final show took place on 25 September at Irvine Meadows Amphitheatre in California (once again, UK fans had to travel to London, with four shows at Earls Court the only ones undertaken this time out). Again, seven of the eight songs from *Crime Of The Century* were in the set, with 'If Everyone Was Listening' still the one to miss out. Following the song 'From Now On' at that final show, Roger Hodgson made a farewell speech, as it was, by now, common knowledge that he was leaving – amusingly, the band then presented him with a gold watch! Perhaps fittingly, the final two songs performed by this lineup, as the encore at that show, were 'School' and 'Crime Of The Century'. Only four songs from *...Famous Last Words...* were performed.

And Then There Were Four – Supertramp Post-Hodgson

Following Roger Hodgson's departure at the end of the 1983 tour, the rest of the band made no secret of their determination to go on without him, believing that they still had plenty to say as a band. In fact, in the short term, it appeared that the split might have cleared some negative energy and helped both sides, as the subsequent first album releases from both Hodgson and the slimmed-down Supertramp were both excellent pieces of work.

Roger Hodgson got out of the gate first in October 1984 with his album *In The Eye Of The Storm*, a tremendous mix of his commercial sensibilities along with some weightier tendencies returning to his writing, which many still believe to be his finest solo work. Four of the album's seven tracks exceed seven minutes, with the twin highlights of the opening 'Had A Dream (Sleeping With The Enemy)' and the closing 'Only Because Of You' both nearing the nine-minute mark. The proggier wing of the Supertramp support were largely enthused by this, and the songs had the facility to 'breathe' as they eased through the generous runtimes. In fact, the release was reportedly originally planned for some time earlier and to be titled *Sleeping With The Enemy* but was scrapped and redone by Roger before release, as he didn't feel it was good or representative enough in its original form. In 2012, Roger confirmed the details of this to me: 'Yes, you're correct, I did record an album at that time which I wasn't happy with, so it got scrapped. About half of the contents went on to get redone and released later, but the rest won't see the light of day, I think it's safe to say. It wasn't up to the standard I wanted.'

Supertramp, meanwhile, headed back into the studio in 1984 to record their own first post-Hodgson album, *Brother Where You Bound*, which was released in May 1985. This was, in fact, a bold statement by the new incarnation of the band, as it featured a much more overtly 'progressive' direction, including not only the eight-minute opener 'Cannonball' (a US hit single in edited form) but also the 16-minute title track, which occupied most of the second side of vinyl. A weighty tale of cold-war tensions and the like (apt considering his and Hodgson's very own private 'cold war'), the track was an undoubted highlight, but, in fact, the truth of the matter was that it had originally been slated for inclusion on what became ... *Famous Last Words...* but was abandoned. As Roger Hodgson told me in 2012:

I didn't follow them that closely, though I was aware of what they were doing, of course. For me, it wasn't really Supertramp anymore – it was Rick. I left him the name, and he trademarked it, so now Supertramp is basically Rick and whatever group of musicians he chooses to use. He could put together a whole bunch of plumbers and go out as Supertramp if he wanted! Interestingly, though, a lot of the songs on *Brother Where You Bound* were things we had been working on before I left. The title track and 'Cannonball' were two of the things which we had wanted to put on ...*Famous Last Words*... if the band had been unified enough, so that gives an idea of how much stronger that album could have been. They were Rick's songs, certainly, so they were his to use, but a lot of my arrangement ideas were in there.

The album, it must be said, stands up as one of Supertramp's very best, and along with Roger's *In The Eye Of The Storm*, an unexpected triumph. It did suffer from a bland and dull cover design, so typical of the 1980s, featuring the famous 'ape into human' 'Ascent Of Man' illustration in gaudily coloured silhouettes on a stark white background. However, it also notably had an inner sleeve showing the four band members walking in a line in a way which bears an astonishingly close resemblance to the later and more well-known Genesis illustration for 'I Can't Dance'. Of course, both arguably take a cue from *Abbey Road*, so perhaps there is little which is truly new.

The real issues between Davies and Hodgson really began when Supertramp resumed touring following the album. There had been an agreement between the two that neither would play the other's songs, an edict which Hodgson has stuck to until the present day, but this was, of course, far more tricky for a band under the Supertramp banner to stick to, with audiences not unrealistically wanting and expecting to hear 'the hits'. To be fair to Davies, the band did play the whole 90-date *Brother On The Road* tour without a single one of Roger's songs, but by all accounts, there was a notable amount of audience dissatisfaction. By the time the next tour came along (following 1987's very disappointing *Free As A Bird* album, which retreated almost entirely from the proggier direction), Davies had relented to pressure and put the odd song, such as 'The Logical Song', 'Breakfast In America' and 'School', into the set. He maintained that the decision to exclude Roger's songs had been an artistic one, owing to his distinctive vocal, but this only served to greatly worsen the tensions between them. Speaking to me in 2012, Roger reiterated the fact that he would not play any of Rick's songs in his own shows and – while appreciating the expectation for a Supertramp show to feature 'the hits' – once again restated the position as he saw it:

No, I think it would be totally wrong to include any of Rick's material. I mean, Rick shouldn't be doing any of mine; that was the agreement, but I could never feature any of his songs. I barely have enough time to fit in all the ones of mine that I want to, anyway! Yes, of course, I understand the pressure Rick is under, but he knew that at the time when he first agreed not to feature my songs. That was the condition by which I agreed to give him the name – I mean, I'm not great at business, but I'm not stupid! Unfortunately, that agreement didn't hold, but it is what it is, and I just want to showcase my songs in the concerts that I'm doing.

Roger and Rick did work together briefly in 1993, firstly with John Helliwell at an event in honour of Jerry Moss of A&M Records, performing 'The Logical Song' and 'Goodbye Stranger', and subsequently, on demo recordings of the songs 'You Win, I Lose' and 'And The Light'. This did not work out, however, and when the songs were eventually used in 1997 on the newly reformed Supertramp's album *Some Things Never Change*, they were without any of Roger's input. There was reportedly some discussion concerning a full reunion, including live performances, but these negotiations were never satisfactorily resolved, and talks broke down without a successful resolution being found. Some reports have claimed that part of the reason for this was the fact that Rick's wife Sue was the band's manager, and Roger found it a difficult prospect to go up against 'two Davieses'. It is possible that things could have progressed had Sue stepped aside as band manager, but Rick was, perhaps understandably, not receptive to the idea. What did occur a little before that time, however, in 1990, was that Roger Hodgson was approached by Yes to replace Jon Anderson as lead vocalist, as Anderson had departed to form the Anderson Bruford Wakeman Howe collective towards the end of the 1980s. He declined, but the prospect remains an intriguing one, and he did, in fact, co-write the song 'Walls', which appeared on the 1994 Yes album *Talk*.

Supertramp, meanwhile, had effectively disbanded following the 1988 tour and did not reconvene until 1996, this time down to a core trio without Dougie Thompson, but bringing Mark Hart – who had been an integral part of the band as an unofficial member throughout the 1980s – into the official lineup. Bob Siebenberg's son Jesse also joined in 1997, by which time, the band were an eight-piece. Following the release of *Some Things Never Change* and the live *It Was The Best Of Times* in 1997, 2002's *Slow Motion* proved to be the last album of new Supertramp material, and interestingly, included the previously unrecorded song 'Goldrush', which used to open the band's shows back in the pre-*Crime Of The Century* era. It has been heavily speculated that the song was co-written with Roger Hodgson, but on the album, it was credited only to Davies and Richard Palmer.

There has been talk of a further rumour of reunion attempts around 2005, but if this is the case, nothing materialised. What is known, however, is that when Supertramp announced a major tour for 2010, Roger Hodgson did make an offer to perform at selected shows with the band. This offer was rebuffed as no reply was ever forthcoming, and the door was effectively closed on any reunion from that point.

Supertramp planned on another tour in 2015, but this was cancelled owing to Rick requiring medical treatment as he was suffering from myeloma. He has reportedly recovered at the time of writing, but as yet, there has been no further Supertramp activity, whether live or recorded, so one might assume that the band's activity is now effectively in its past. Roger Hodgson, by contrast, has continued to work quite extensively in a touring capacity, crisscrossing much of the world on a couple of lengthy excursions as he continues to celebrate the music that he created with Supertramp, as well as highlights from his own solo catalogue (he released the album *Hai-Hai* in 1987 and the widely acclaimed *Open The Door* in 2000, along with a couple of excellent live albums).

Crime Of The Century had its 40th anniversary in 2014, which was marked by the release of an 'Anniversary' deluxe edition featuring a show recorded on the original *Crime* tour at Hammersmith. A little before that, in 2012, came the long hoped-for release of the *Live In Paris* 79 DVD, featuring the filmed footage of the *Paris* live album material. There was some disagreement about this release, with neither Davies nor Hodgson having any input into the making or quality of the release, but Roger Hodgson, at least, was sanguine about it following the release, telling me in 2012:

> There really isn't any other footage that I know of that exists of that classic lineup, which is a shame. I'm glad it came out, actually, so that the fans have something as a snapshot of the band at its peak; the unhappiness I had was from being shut out of the creative

process. Rick and I had no input at all, and I think fans of the band would have enjoyed what we could have contributed in terms of bonus material, the stories behind the songs, that sort of thing. So, it's annoying that it could have been so much better, and I'd have loved for it to be, but unfortunately, that wasn't an option.

A refreshingly balanced take on the release I believe, as there have been far too many examples of much-anticipated releases being forever blocked because of disagreements and legal red tape. Perfect the DVD may not have been, but it still constitutes a marvellously entertaining complement to the live album and it is wonderful to see the band in full flight – and, of course, still performing seven out of the eight songs from the *Crime Of The Century* album. The show was reissued in 2015 as an expanded 2DVD plus 2CD set, with some earlier crediting errors corrected, so things were, at least, improved.

If this is really, as it would certainly appear, the end of Supertramp as a band, then it becomes more natural than ever to look back at the legacy they gave us at their peak. And for many, that peak will always remain *Crime Of The Century*. In terms of the casual listener, the hits which immediately come to mind will generally be 'The Logical Song', 'Breakfast In America' and probably 'It's Raining Again'. This is natural and to be expected, as they come from a period when Supertramp had become a household name and no strangers to the singles chart. The whole package of *Breakfast In America*, with the image, the timing and the radio-friendly songs, was a marketing man's dream, and it is no surprise – and certainly fully deserved – that it made the impression it did and continues to do.

However, the genuine Supertramp fan will be different. Just like all successful bands, dedicated fans will gravitate towards deeper cuts and albums with real substance to them. Fans of Zeppelin will go to 'Kashmir' and 'Achilles Last Stand' rather than 'Stairway To Heaven' and 'Whole Lotta Love'. Deep Purple aficionados will take 'Child In Time' or 'Burn' over 'Smoke On The Water'. Fans of The Who will often gravitate away from *Tommy* and towards the real meat of *Quadrophenia*. And so it is with Supertramp – and while *Even In The Quietest Moments,* in particular, has remained a favourite of a good number of the more 'prog'-minded fanbase, there is something about *Crime Of The Century* in which (no pun intended) all of the stars aligned: the music was meticulously arranged and flawlessly cohesive, with real depth to it on repeated listening. The lineup was suddenly there to give the band its full potential, and yet, also still fresh and exciting, working as a team and all pulling in the same direction without friction. And lastly, the whole package, with the iconic album cover image, gives just the right note of synchronous mystery and fascination.

When the roll call of classic 20th century rock albums is made, *Crime Of The Century* should always be present, correct and in the front rank. It was, and remains, what it deserves.

Bibliography

Shenton, L., *The Logical Book: A Supertramp Compendium* (Wymer, 2020)

Melhuish, M., *The Supertramp Book* (Omnibus, 1986)

Fuentes, A., *Tramp's Footprints: The History of Supertramp* (UNO, 2021)